D0926661

BEEN THERE, RUN THAT

Edited and Introduced
by Kay Koplovitz

A Springboard Enterprises® Book

Rosetta Press
NEW YORK 2014

BEEN THERE, RUN THAT

© 2014 Springboard 2000 Enterprises, Inc.

Preface, chapter introductions and takeaways © 2014 Kay Koplovitz

Much of the material collected in this book previously appeared, sometimes in different form, in article or blog form.

All rights reserved. No part of this book may be used or reproduced in any form or by any electronic or mechanical means, including information storage and retrieval systems, without permission in writing from the publisher, except by a reviewer who may quote brief passages in a review.

All of the author's net proceeds from this project will benefit Springboard Enterprises®.

Cover design by Jay McNair
Interior design by Brehanna Ramirez

Published 2014 by Rosetta Press
ISBN: 978-0-795-34489-3

The following material is original to this volume:
"How to Move Your Product to Market: Sweet Advice from Sweetriot," copyright © 2013 Sarah Endline; "Ten Things You Should Know about Term Sheets for Equity Financing," copyright © 2014 Ellen Corenswet; "An Appreciation of Muriel 'Mickie' Siebert (1928–2013)," copyright © 2014 Amy Millman

Copyright page information continues on page 249.

For Mickie Siebert
who opened a big door
and expected us all to walk through

CONTENTS

iv

O N JANUARY 27, 2000, Springboard Enterprises was officially launched into the venture capital community with our first forum at the Oracle Conference Center in Redwood City, California. That day, the first twenty-six companies stepped onto the stage in the very first venture forum featuring women entrepreneurs who came to raise venture capital for their technology businesses. As I stood on stage to introduce Springboard presenters, a nervous energy rippled through the room.

Some there must have been wondering what we were thinking. Venture capitalists barely knew any women founders who could drive growth. Yes, there were some women leading large and growing corporations, Carly Fiorina at Hewlett Packard and Meg Whitman at eBay among them. But this was different. Our women were founders and determined to scale their businesses in technology, media, e-commerce and biotech. No one had even heard of these businesses and their women founders but all had rich expertise and certainly the ability to build successful businesses.

My partner Amy Millman and I had reached out through every university alumnae association, every women's business organization, every personal contact each of the cofounders of Springboard had access to and more. Every founder had been coached by a team handpicked to strengthen business models, management teams and, most important, had been schooled in giving presentations geared to investors. The women were great students of the process and this day was graduating day.

It was showtime—a chance for them to present in front of an audience of five hundred investors.

Krishna Subramanian, founder of Kovair, was first up. We had a lot of confidence in her. A software engineer at Sun Microsystems with five patents to her credit, Krishna had walked out on her stock options to launch Kovair with its patent-pending technology to build custom websites for enterprise businesses. I loved her quiet self-confidence, her presentation style and her ability to capture the audience. She had launched her company nine months earlier with $1.5 million and was there seeking $8 million to $10 million in growth capital. She was twenty-nine.

Krishna opened her presentation with a play on a familiar quote from Shakespeare: "To B2B, or not to B2B? That is the question." She explained why she chose to offer her service to enterprise companies instead of consumers. She clicked through her clear and concise B2B presentation without a hitch. The audience was attentive. You could see they were thinking that maybe, just maybe, these companies would stack up against the rigorous benchmarks set by the venture investors. They ultimately rewarded her with a $9 million investment, and Kovair took off.

Being a self-described futurist, I seldom reflect on my career, but compiling this book has brought me back to how this all began. I have the experience of founding and building a multibillion-dollar company, USA Networks, and I knew women could hold their own in a fully competitive world.

Springboard faced the challenge of finding women with the talent, drive, experience and vision to build these scalable companies. The year we began to mount our effort, 1999, over $100 billion in venture capital was invested, yet only 1.7 percent went to women.

There have been many experiences in my life that influenced me to think big, reach higher and achieve success. Something happened in 1999, though, that left a profound impression on me and on our ability to achieve for women entrepreneurs so much more than was ever expected.

In 1999, the national women's soccer team electrified the nation when it claimed the World Cup by defeating the team from China in a tense shoot-out. Over ninety thousand screaming fans at the Rose Bowl in Pasadena on July 10 danced in the stands as Brandi Chastain scored the winning point beyond the reach of the Chinese goaltender. Over forty million watched the event on TV, at the time the largest audience for World Cup soccer, men's or women's.

The victory was sweet, but the story took place years earlier when the soccer federation decided it would have to start with fundamentals to build a team for ultimate success. Coach Bruce Arena scoured the nation for middle school and high school girls with great potential. Mia Hamm, at thirteen, was among the youngest. The players came from all different ethnic backgrounds and geographic locations, and they came to learn to play as a team.

Years of coaching went into bringing this team together, scouting talent, training, coaching and getting out onto the field to be challenged in national and international competition. Years of hard work by hundreds of people supporting these players came together to seize victory that day in July 1999.

What Springboard faced in 1999 putting our team together was nothing short of what women's soccer did to achieve success in that year. We had to start from the beginning, finding the talent, bringing them together, coaching them, giving them a place to play and in the end access to resources to achieve success. There were many doubters, but not among us.

This is what I want for entrepreneurs, especially for women: to believe in themselves, to dream bigger, reach higher, to achieve success beyond their wildest expectations. That's why Springboard was founded. That's why we've assembled our entrepreneurial experts and asked them to spill their stories, their lessons, their advice onto these pages.

Now fifteen years later the realization of this vision is proof that there is remarkable know-how within our network of human capital and in the thesis that investing in women is smart business. Over five hundred fifty women-led companies have been through the Springboard accelerator programs. More than 80 percent of these companies raise capital, and more than 80 percent are in business as of this writing, either in their original form or as a part of mergers or acquisition. Eleven companies completed IPOs. The women entrepreneurs who founded and lead these companies are highly educated and high-performing professionals and are no longer the best-kept secret.

Even entrepreneurs in the midlife of their companies can find sage advice on issues they never contemplated when they started out. Students who are filling courses on entrepreneurship at colleges and universities will find value in real-life advice from those who have truly "been there, run that." We hope you will find these articles, organized by theme, useful quick tips to guide you in your business decisions. Springboard offers these in hope that by peeling back the veil of mystery to raising capital and building scalable businesses, we are helping more women achieve economic parity.

I am grateful to all of the women and men whose articles are in this anthology, for their selfless contribution to the benefit of others. It is very much in keeping with the pledge of our entrepreneurs who have benefited from our human capital network to pay it forward to those who choose the same path.

Kay Koplovitz
New York City
September 2014

ONE: STARTING UP

O NE OF THE HARDEST DECISIONS aspiring entrepreneurs have to make is deciding when to start up. It's not always so easy to know. One must ask: What's my product or service? Does it solve a problem? When do I leave my full-time job, or, simply, how do I get started?

Often, when I'm speaking on college campuses, students looking to become the next Mark Zuckerberg ask me how they'll know when an idea is good enough. I recall vividly a class I addressed at the University of British Columbia in 2005 that was focused on business models, and start-up models in particular. Students were searching for signs that they had the "next big thing." They were energetic and inquisitive, and I really enjoyed the dialogue with them. Their eagerness and enthusiasm is the reason I try to make myself available to students on campus. They seek guidance based on real-life experience and are ready to soak up information. Like the Nike slogan, I tell them, "Just do it." It's the only real way to learn.

After this class in Vancouver, a young man came up to me to ask how he'll know it's time to "just do it." I could see by the perplexed look on his face that he had no idea of how to develop the right idea to create a business. To understand a bit of what his interests were, I asked him what he enjoyed doing most. After a short discussion about game apps, I could hear that what drove him was the creative software process. That's when I told him what I believe to be true for entrepreneurs in search of the next big thing: "You'll know when you've got the right idea. It simply will capture your imagination and never let you go."

For those who have full-time positions, it's a hard decision to leave the safety of a regular paycheck and strike out on their own without a safety net. Financial insecurity frightens us all. Every entrepreneur has to know his or her own tolerance for risk, financial and personal. It's an individual decision each person must make. Fortunately, many have found a way to work on their ideas, test the market and develop contacts in the business sector, and to network among others who have already taken the leap, all before they leave a permanent post. There is comfort for many in starting this way. For those in this position, Kelly Fitzsimmons offers advice in her article "Ten Signs You're Ready to Quit Your Day Job."

It is an obsession with an idea that drives people to make the leap into entrepreneurship. Starting a business of your own is not for the faint of heart. Yes, I realize that some start out in business because options for them are limited, or because circumstances have changed within a company, and doing something is better than doing nothing. Whatever the reason, I applaud the ingenuity in creating a lifestyle business. But even then, there must be a real drive to see the product or service through. Competitors abound, whether you're starting up the next great restaurant or the next Angry Birds. If you want to know if your idea has legs, Denise Brosseau offers sound advice in her article "How to Sell Your Ideas."

Many people don't really know how to start up a company, but instead start by working on a hobby part-time while still employed. Good advice for part-time and early-stage companies comes from Ellie Cachette in her article "Bootstrapping: Five Tips." Not ready to leave that full-time job yet? You can still refine your entrepreneurial skills as described by Marcia Zellers's article, "Trapped in a Big Company? What's an Entrepreneur to Do?"

In this first chapter of *Been There, Run That,* founders in our Springboard community share with readers their experiences of starting up. They share ideas from how to bootstrap a start-up on little cash and a lot of sweat equity to sage advice on forming partnerships and how to avoid dangerous pitfalls. I hope their wisdom gives you comfort. Hard-learned lessons are theirs to share.

TEN SIGNS YOU'RE READY TO QUIT YOUR DAY JOB

KELLY FITZSIMMONS

The day job is the bane of many an entrepreneur.
Here are ten signs you're ready to ditch it.

T HAT DAY JOB can be a killer. And often, it's not just that you're itching to work full time on your start-up. It's that the day job is making you miserable all on its own.

We often talk about the Peter Principle, which holds that people get promoted to their level of incompetency. But there is another way, and it's worse. Sometimes, we remain competent but fail in another and worse way. We become lifeless shells of our former selves, persevering in the name of personal growth and development… and hating it all the way.

Here are ten telltale signs that you are ready to leave your day job. Mind you, these are not ten signs that you are ready to be an entrepreneur. But they will tell you that your day job, at least, is not working out.

1. *You've heard yourself say, repeatedly, "The pay just isn't worth it."*
2. *Those nearest to you say you've changed, and not for the better.*

3. *No matter what, you wake at 3 A.M. in a cold sweat, trying to solve a work-related problem.*
4. *When you talk about your job, you get bored, break into a sweat or change the subject.*
5. *You've taken more sick days than vacation in the last year.*
6. *You don't want the day to start, making it a struggle to get out of bed.*
7. *You start fantasizing about a car accident, serious illness or some other event that would put you in the hospital for months, giving you, in effect, a guilt-free vacation.*
8. *You've accepted the fact that you're miserable, but you won't even contemplate leaving because you're worried about what will happen to others if you quit.*
9. *You have persistent nausea or a heightened emotional state most days.*
10. *Before arriving at the office, you take several deep, long breaths to steel yourself for the day—every day.*

If you can see yourself in this list—if many of these resonate with you—you are harming yourself. Harming yourself is failure. You are failing to live a happy and productive life.

One of my most competent friends said that her executive coach had to tell her to quit, repeatedly. She said she needed someone else to validate that it was OK to leave. Well, I'm happy to be that someone else. Print out this list and show it to your boss if you have to. Email me if you want me to sign it.

KAY'S TAKEAWAYS

- The signs are all around you—take notice.
- The most important indicator that you're ready to quit your day job is simply that you don't like waking up to the challenges of the day, whatever they are.

HOW TO SELL YOUR IDEAS
DENISE BROSSEAU

*You've got all your employees excited about your
vision. Now, it's time to convince the rest of the world.*

T O MAKE A DIFFERENCE in your company and your
market, you have to get others to accept and promote your
ideas. You're already a leader in your company. The next step is
to become a leader in your niche—to use your ideas to influence
an entire market, and to help your vision of the future take hold.
As an executive talent agent working with senior executives and
CEOS, I encourage my clients to get out of the office and start
building visibility, credibility and reputation.

I subscribe to the VRE formula for success: Begin with a well-
tested and honed *vision*, accumulate a track record of *executing*
successfully and then get out of the office to build the right
relationships and share your ideas. Here's how to begin.

Vision: Getting out there
Just as you test products before bringing them to market, you
need to test your ideas before trying to become an evangelist for
them. So try explaining the kernel of your big idea to appropriate stakeholders to get their input. Once you're confident that

7

you can get others to understand and accept your basic idea, try reframing it so that it tells a bigger story that engages others.

The next step is to find speaking opportunities that will let you champion your vision. There is an aura of trust around the person on the dais or behind the microphone. That's earned by having something meaningful and memorable to say. Without that invitation to speak outside of our organization, we often don't take the time to gather the evidence and anecdotes that give us credibility and help convert others to our point of view.

Relationships: Why conferences and boards matter
Identifying and nurturing relationships—with investors, advisors and potential employees—will allow you to spread your ideas much more quickly.

Attending conferences and serving on boards are great ways to test and refine your vision, and to meet the people who can make it happen. Start by thinking about the people you want to learn from or influence. Then split them into A and B lists, and identify the people on the A list whom you most need to meet within the next three years. Which events do the A players attend, and which boards are they a part of? Who can help you get the right invitations to those opportunities?

Execution: Your track record
People will remember you and come to rely on you if you do what you say you will do. That's enough to put you ahead of the pack in pretty much every situation.

That does not mean you have to do everything yourself or work 24/7. Sure, it's easy to think, "Oh, I can do this faster (or better) than anyone else." Before you know it, it's 1 A.M. Again.

So make the most of virtual assistants, crowdsourcing, online cloud services and the creation of a "do not do" list.

Deadline: One year
Create a one-page plan—now—that will help you stay focused on the right opportunities to build visibility, credibility and reputation this year.

Then share it with a few of your key supporters and mentors. Why? Well, I was recently asked by one of my champions to refer some candidates for a for-profit board position. I happily forwarded three names. She called me back to say, "What about you? Didn't you have on your one-page plan that you wanted to join a for-profit board this year?" Oops! Yes, I did. But it had never occurred to me to put my name forward. And yes, now that part of my plan has become a reality.

KAY'S TAKEAWAYS

- Understand your concept and refine your pitch, then find opportunities to speak about it in order to create visibility.
- Do what you say you will do, so make strategic choices for what to agree to.
- Know when to say no thanks, or not right now.
- Create a plan, vet it with your supporters, set deadlines and then take credit for your successes!

BOOTSTRAPPING: FIVE TIPS

ELLIE CACHETTE

Bootstrapping means managing your time
as closely as your money. Here's how to do it.

WHILE VENTURE-BACKED TECH START-UPS seem to get all the press, there are many, many ways to start your company. Some entrepreneurs do it while hanging on to their day jobs full time. Some use the money they've saved to give themselves a defined runway (i.e., I get six months to accomplish these three things; otherwise, I move on). Others seem to rely exclusively on hustle and luck. Here's what I've learned about one of the less glamorous forms of funding: bootstrapping.

1. Press
Having press access can get you far. Knowing the right people or having access to conferences and parties can sometimes be all that it takes to make a life-changing connection. Try to get as many speaking or writing events as possible. How is that possible early on? Start small, think about something you know about, and work from there. Know only about exotic turtles? Blog about turtles. Find a blog about turtles and guest post. Try to get a free pass to a turtle conference. There's nothing the world loves more than experts. You have to start somewhere.

2. Time

In the beginning, you will think that there is a competitor secretly working in the middle of the night ready to steal your idea. But the start-up game is not necessarily about being fastest or first to market. It's about being smarter.

- Time will be your most limited resource.
- Block off chunks of time for certain things so you are not wasting energy moving from place to place.
- Leave mornings open for operational chores. Preserve afternoons for face-to-face meetings.

3. Travel cheaply

Traveling cheaply is an art and starts with a great network and a smart approach.

- Keep your travel dates flexible, bite the bullet on layovers, and build loyalty miles in as many ways as possible.
- Couches are your friend. They are cheap and give you time to catch up with friends and colleagues in ways you normally wouldn't. Upon first arriving in New York, I stayed on a very influential entrepreneur's couch. Not only did I have a comfy place to sleep, but I learned a lot about the community and launching a start-up just from midnight chats.

4. Advisors

Advisors can be a source of "free" or equity-only expert advice. Without a retainer or hourly billing rate, you can get top-notch ideas and support without feeling the burden of a big bill. Many times start-ups search for advisors who "look good" on paper, but early on, that may not be what you need. Look for people who are available part-time, but are still accessible for those company-changing decisions.

5. Community
As an entrepreneur, giving back—at all times and in whatever way you can—should be your No. 1 job. Funding and money are glamorized by the media, but to reach your milestones you will need support from your community. Need more users or testers? Community. Need to find that cofounder or advisor? Community. Are you a hardcore coder? Build a friend a widget. Are you a master marketer? Help another start-up with a campaign.

Above all, the key to bootstrapping is being creative. Get the most done with the least and keep a smile on your face. Bootstrapping is about never counting on funding. Funding is a mysterious and weird animal that is difficult to predict. Odd as it sounds, many entrepreneurs will tell you that some of their favorite memories are from back in the day when times were lean. Enjoy it, because one day you might get that big funding or bring in senior executives. Before you know it, those nights on friends' couches will seem too far away.

- When running a company on very little money (bootstrapping), guard your time—your most limited resource—as closely as your cash. Prioritize.
- Establish yourself as an expert to gain visibility and use all media.
- Build your human capital network (mentors, press, community). It will pay off.

WHERE ARE ALL THE WOMEN ENTREPRENEURS?
DENISE BROSSEAU

Sure, women start lots of companies. But where are the big, world-changing businesses run by women?

I GET THIS QUESTION all the time: Where are all the women entrepreneurs? I guess the people who ask figure I should know: I'm the cofounder of the Forum for Women Entrepreneurs and cofounder of the Springboard Venture Forums, and I've helped women raise over $5 billion for their businesses.

My response is simple: Statistics show that women in the U.S. start companies at a very brisk pace compared to their male counterparts. The question that remains interesting—and is less frequently asked—is why are so few women starting big companies? Even women who have started businesses that get outside funding do not tend to end up with businesses as large as those run by men.

After more than twenty years of meeting with, advising and learning from women entrepreneurs, I believe that women either do not like or do not feel comfortable spinning a big vision.

An incremental business will not change the world.

If you are seeking outside funding, you are asking potential investors to put money into your idea above all others. To do that, you need a big vision. Most people are inspired to invest in big ideas that can change the world instead of small, incremental ideas that will likely happen without their help. If you have dollars to put to work, wouldn't you be more excited to be able to say you are funding the next SpaceX or iRobot or Zipcar (the latter two were cofounded by women, incidentally) rather than another small services firm? I would.

But something happens when women put together their investor pitch or think critically about their businesses. They actually want to understand exactly how they are going to get from Point A to Point Z and they want to explain to an investor the steps (B, C, D) they will take and exactly how they will spend the money they raise.

This sounds like a good thing, but it pushes the entrepreneur to think small, and to designate their Point Z as only a few steps into the future and on a path that is clearly visible to all. In most cases, this is neither exciting nor inspiring. It is just an incremental business that will not change the world.

Robin Chase, cofounder of Zipcar, tells the story of her meeting with the dean of MIT's Sloan School of Management (of which she is an alumna) to get his input on her business idea. After he saw her pitch, he got very excited, but he immediately pushed her to think much bigger. She recalls sitting down with her cofounder in a coffee shop at the meeting. The two just looked at each other... shocked and a bit scared. Could they do it? *Should* they do it? After a lot of soul searching, they did, and Zipcar was born.

Work backward from the future.

If we're going to see a change in the number of big businesses founded by women, they will have to get comfortable spinning a much bigger story. They'll have to ask themselves questions like:

- What if I had ten times the amount of money I am asking for; what would I do with it?
- If we could really dream big about changing this industry/niche, what would we do?
- What's the "What If?" future we'd like to bring about?

Then, work backward from those possibilities to clarify the broad strokes and milestones that need to be met to get there. It isn't about smoke and mirrors. It is about admitting that you don't know every step that lies ahead of you, and trusting that you'll figure it out.

Get help from those who have come before you.

There is a funny dance in this start-up process that often feels very uncomfortable. We have to push ourselves to think big and then not become so overwhelmed by the big idea that we get stopped in our tracks. It is important to ask for help, to surround yourself with big thinkers and others who are ahead of you on the start-up path, and to constantly test and verify your assumptions. And, as women, don't just talk to other women. Find some men who can serve as advisors, too.

Women are the key drivers of the economy. We should also be the leaders that create the solutions to the world's big problems and lead the companies that bring those solutions to market. If we can conquer this big vision challenge, I believe we are poised to do just that, and to change the world forever.

KAY'S TAKEAWAYS

- The best ideas are transformational, not incremental.
- Women need to envision the future, then start from scratch to work toward executing the vision without having all the answers first.
- Surround yourself with the best thinkers.

HOW TO WRITE A PRE-NUP FOR YOUR PARTNERSHIP

LAURA MCCANN RAMSEY

Sure, everything seems rosy now. But when you and your cofounder no longer see eye to eye, you'll be glad you did the paperwork early on.

E NTREPRENEURSHIP IS NOT for the faint of heart. Many of us, understandably, want a partner or cofounder at our side. But after twenty years, four companies and six partners, I've learned that partnering doesn't solve everything, and often introduces its own difficulties. Here are six rules that will help you set the groundwork for a great partnership—and a decent breakup, should you need one.

Imagine "the end."
Don't agree to partner with anyone, or take on a partner, until you are clear in your own mind and on paper about how you would choose to end your business. The partnership agreement is going to be the equivalent of your business pre-nup, and now is the time to think about what happens in the event of a separation or divorce. Your buy-sell and partnership agreements should clearly spell out every potential scenario.

Just having this conversation will reveal more about your potential partner then you could ever imagine—or maybe more than you want to know. The best partnerships are built around clear and specific roles, operational guidelines and legal contracts.

Tough talk, not love talk

At the beginning, it's great to be in love with your partner. Your partner will undoubtedly be the person you spend the most time with, share secrets with and grow your business with—unless you grow to hate them. Have tough conversations before committing, and explore every possible relationship and business outcome you can think of: What if you work harder? What if they work smarter? What if they bring in the money? What if it was your idea? What if your partner wants to leave? What if the investors want only one of you to stay? Good partnerships set the foundation for a better breakup with honest, open communication. No scenario is too uncomfortable to consider. Anything can happen, and it probably will.

Who's the boss?

Don't gloss over your job descriptions. Think of the contingencies: You swap roles, one of you steps away or a family matter takes all your attention. Can your buy-sell agreement handle all of these?

Review your job descriptions every six months, and keep them updated. Working on your partnership is part of your job. Make it part of your mission statement.

The paper trail

Every partnership should be built one document at a time. Don't skip over any details, even if they seem like a pain in the neck at the time. And put it all in writing, especially your concerns.

Keep a paper trail. Print everything important and relevant to the pulse of your relationship and put these documents in a file. You might not like to think about it now, but when you most need this information, you may not have access to your computer or company email.

My attorney
If you and your partner get into a dispute, your company's attorney can't take sides and shouldn't. So when things get tense, your partner's attorney will be sitting across the table. You need your own personal attorney. You need someone who not only understands how to build businesses, but has experience closing them down.

When you meet with your attorney, skip the storytelling—you're paying by the hour. Just get clear on your legal standing, and what you can and can't do to get your partnership on track or end it.

The partnership advisory board
While the ultimate decision about who to take on as a partner is yours alone, you still need a personal set of advisors. These can be your attorney, entrepreneurs who have been through partnerships themselves or a life partner—who probably knows more about your partnership than anyone else. These are the folks who will watch your back and can help you decide whether to love, mediate or leave your partnership.

Ultimately, you are accountable for everything about your business, even picking your partner. So choose wisely and prepare that pre-nup.

KAY'S TAKEAWAYS

- In the beginning, imagine the end. Create the agreements and a plan in case you need to dissolve the partnership in the future.

- Set up ground rules with well-defined roles and operating agreements as well as legal contracts to support them.

- Document important conversations, as well as concerns, and keep copies off-premises in case you are not able to access the office.

TRAPPED IN A BIG COMPANY?
WHAT'S AN ENTREPRENEUR TO DO?

MARCIA ZELLERS

Here's how to become an entrepreneur-in-residence—
even if that isn't your official title.

AT SOME TIME in your career, you're likely to be an entrepreneur trapped inside a large corporation. Unless you've
sold your last company and have a fat bank account, the reasons for this are probably financial—you've got kids to support
and a mortgage to pay. What's an entrepreneur-at-heart to
do? Feed your soul and aid your company by becoming an
entrepreneur-in-residence.

In the classic sense, I've been an entrepreneur twice—first in
1999, then in 2008. You'll notice that in both cases, my timing
was perfect: for an economic meltdown. While incubating my
next passion—Tootzypop, a daily blog, email and community
for women over forty—I'm working as an entrepreneur-in-
residence at FIDM/Fashion Institute of Design & Merchandising, where I head the digital marketing department. I run
my group as if it were my own business. I get big ideas, better
returns and more motivated employees by practicing the
following:

Pretend you work in a start-up.
Don't think of yourself as a cog. You're the start-up CEO of whatever you control at your company. Ask yourself how you might do your job differently if you applied the zeal and wiliness of a start-up CEO day-to-day. Take a risk, do things differently, have an uncompromising belief that you will succeed, and you'll be surprised at how differently you'll approach your work.

Encourage inspiration.
Young, entrepreneurial companies are often cash-strapped, but they offer their employees the opportunity to be a part of something rich with possibility. Even within a big company, you can create ways for your team to inspire and be inspired:

- Encourage new ideas and create a forum for your employees to share them publicly.
- Host an innovation summit, and charge your team with investigating and reporting on the cutting edge of your industry. Then brainstorm related innovations for your business.
- Send your staff to conferences that are outside their direct functional area but that will infuse them with new ideas and motivation. (Don't forget to send yourself!)
- Never be afraid that an employee's ideas will overshadow your own. Their great ideas are an indication that you are indeed fostering the right entrepreneurial spirit.

Start a side project.

Chances are you've got a few new business ideas brewing. Yes, that full-time job takes up most of your time—but most likely you can squeeze a few extra hours out of the week.

Don't feel you need to launch a full-fledged company right away: Break your idea down into manageable chunks and start with what you think is doable. Slowly add additional elements as you're able.

If your idea is successful, you'll experience an entrepreneurial high that will motivate you to squeeze a few more hours out of your week. It might even give you the courage and the means to take it on full time. If it doesn't work, that's good experience, too: For serial entrepreneurs, failure is a badge of honor, proof of their ability to embrace risk. Whether you succeed or fail, you'll acquire new skills.

Accept failure.

Entrepreneurs are idea people who cultivate an environment of experimentation. Young companies also tend to have flatter hierarchical structures and easy access to the CEO, which can promote camaraderie and openness. In the best of these environments, new ideas can flourish. It's accepted that many won't work, but that they may still lead to valuable new products, patents or business processes.

Encourage your team to try new ideas. Expect a certain failure rate, and make sure those who fail are rewarded for the effort rather than punished for a disappointing outcome.

Set aggressive benchmarks.

Most young companies feel capable of great things, and they set goals accordingly. If they've taken venture capital, they're under even more intense pressure to set and meet aggressive milestones. Whether you're a department of one or many, write an ambitious but doable "business plan" that holds you and your team to a higher standard. Be specific and measureable about how you plan to reach these more aggressive goals, and make sure everyone understands their role. Cap it off with an "executive summary" that clearly explains what your charge is as a department or organization, what your new goals are, and how you'll reach them. Give everyone in your department a copy of the plan and have them review it often.

To me, "entrepreneur" is a personal quality as much as it is a business status. If you truly want to be one, most likely you will find a way to make it your title and lifestyle. Meanwhile, you can get a lot of satisfaction for yourself, and mileage for your company, out of an entrepreneurial approach to your current career.

KAY'S TAKEAWAYS

- It is possible to function as an entrepreneur within a large organization.
- Work as if you run a start-up, and encourage the exchange of new ideas within your department.
- Create a comprehensive and challenging business plan; review it with your stakeholders often, and don't be afraid to fail.

TWO: LEADERSHIP

A H, LEADERSHIP! AMAZON ALONE LISTS thirty thousand titles on the subject, and there are thousands more on related topics, including leadership skills, habits of most successful leaders, leading in the time of change and leadership attributes. What's an entrepreneur to do? Many of these topics are interesting and some are useful, but the start-up world is different than the one a CEO of a Fortune 500 company faces. What leadership qualities will you need to start up and sustain your business?

This is what our entrepreneurs address in Chapter Two. I've often observed that relatively new entrepreneurs plunge in and don't think so much about leading others. At most, they look for a few trusted souls, classmates or former colleagues to get the ball rolling. There is so much more than pulling a few people together to being a successful leader.

I have been asked by a number of people writing articles and books what it takes to lead. How did I get into a position of leadership? There is no easy answer. I sometimes feel it's a bit like asking for the definition of pornography: I don't know exactly how to define it, but I know it when I see it.

I do know that the sense that one is a leader happens over time. My first realization came to me early, when my classmates selected me to be the publisher of the fifth-grade newspaper. Believe me, I had no illusions about being William Randolph

Hearst. What I did know was that we had to write the articles, pay for copying them on the mimeograph machine and sell the paper to our fellow students. Our goal was to make enough money to pay for the class trip, no small task. I may have been the only person who would accept the responsibility for doing this.

Meeting my fifth-grade challenge led me to another in the ninth grade, when I was elected to be the announcer for the high school assembly. This was no small task either, as it meant having to engage the audience of ninth- through twelfth-graders, some twelve hundred students, to quiet down and pay attention to the afternoon programs. From this experience, I learned the power of my own voice and the artful use of the microphone.

From here, others came to expect that I'd step up to the plate. Ambition and ability intersected, and others knew leadership when they saw it. I was the valedictorian of my high school graduating class, and was voted most likely to succeed. Perhaps I just wanted it more than other students, and perhaps self-confidence helped me too.

I mention these factors that led me to become a leader in business because I really think these skills are learned along the way. People don't just show up and become leaders, though I do believe the ability to lead lives in all of us. I've been surprised in situations of high stress in business and life. Some people you would never think of as leaders in the group were the ones who stepped forward. They somehow got the "call" for leadership, the kind they possessed, which makes me believe we all have this ability under the right conditions.

The description of an effective leader has changed over the years. Qualities such as decisiveness, authority and strength are giving way to more collaborative attributes such as fairness, transparency, inclusiveness and mutual respect, among many other traits. So what it takes to lead is changing. Leaders still have to lead, but how they lead is changing with the times.

From Erika Andersen, you can learn about developing followers in "Lead So Others Will Follow: Six Tips," and from Laura Strong you can learn about time management in her article "Why 'Urgent' Is Not a Priority." Learn more about time management in "Get More Time to Think," by AlexAnndra Ontra, who cites some of the same thinking found in Daniel Kahneman's book, *Thinking, Fast and Slow*. Bettina Hein addresses with frankness an issue for women in her article, "How to Be Pregnant and CEO: Five Tips."

We are learning every day that people lead differently and that there is not one way to lead. We are also learning that women lead with different strengths from men. Neither is a better model, but as John Gerzema and Michael D'Antonio point out in their book *The Athena Doctrine: How Women (and the Men Who Think Like Them) Will Rule the Future,* the attributes women have, including those of trust, transparency, inclusion and loyalty, are favored by workers around the globe. More on this can be found in my article "Leadership Requires More Feminine Attributes."

In the end, each of us must develop our own leadership qualities. As Bill George wrote in his book *True North: Discover Your Authentic Leadership,* leadership must be authentic. To be effective leaders, we must know our core values and our mission, and we must convey these in the most transparent way to gain the trust and following of others.

LEAD SO OTHERS WILL FOLLOW: SIX TIPS

ERIKA ANDERSEN

No matter what kind of leader you hope to be,
you need to get people behind you. Here's how.

IN THE EARLY YEARS of a business, it's easy to neglect—or even forget entirely—the importance of being a leader. A friend of mine who started a consulting business fell into just this trap. He had a clear idea of what he wanted to do, and worked hard to make it happen, but it never really got off the ground. He and his partner weren't aligned. He hired people who didn't understand what was expected, and then didn't deliver properly. My friend put almost all his energy into logistics and dealing with clients. He didn't lead his organization.

In contrast, the most successful entrepreneurs I know recognize that they have two jobs: Build the business, and lead the people. Even if you only have a few employees, it's important to be a leader to whom they'll commit.

We've found that people look for six characteristics in deciding whether to align around a leader. "Followable" leaders are far-sighted, passionate, courageous, wise, generous and trustworthy. Here's what that looks like in the day-to-day of entrepreneurial life:

- Being *far-sighted* means you see and share a clear and compelling vision of the future with your people—staff, partners, investors. You see past obstacles and difficulties and focus on moving toward the future you all want to create.
- As a *passionate* leader, your followers know what you stand for, and that you'll stick to your guns even when the going gets tough. At the same time, you're open to hearing their questions and concerns. You are committed without being dogmatic.
- Being *courageous* means you make tough, necessary decisions even when doing so is uncomfortable or risky. And if a decision turns out badly, you'll take full responsibility: Admit your mistakes, apologize and work to fix what's wrong.
- Being *wise* means you combine curiosity and objectivity. Your team can come to you for counsel, because they know that you're reflective about important decisions and that you learn from your mistakes.
- As a *generous leader,* you believe in your folks, provide balanced feedback, share credit and teach what you know. As a result, your people can take on bigger and bigger roles in helping you grow the business.
- Being *trustworthy* makes you a rock and a haven for your followers. They know you'll always do your best to tell them the truth and to keep confidences. And they know, too, that you'll do everything possible to get the results you promise.

It's easy, when you're starting a business, to think that leadership isn't that important. Your staff is small, you're all in it together, and you're focused on just-getting-this-thing-off-the-ground. But in some ways, this is the most important time to show your leadership. This is when you can build a foundation of being the kind of leader to whom people turn and say, "I'm with you—let's go."

KAY'S TAKEAWAYS

- It's easy to get busy with the day-to-day logistics of running of a company, but establishing leadership is one of the main priorities successful entrepreneurs get busy with.
- Define expectations, align goals and don't assume that everyone working hard will replace good leadership.
- Bring your vision, passion, courage, wisdom and generosity and be trustworthy—your people will follow!

HOW TO LEAD FROM THE MIDDLE
KAY KOPLOVITZ

You may think a good leader needs to be out in front.
Not always.

HAVING BEEN THE FOUNDER and CEO of USA Networks for more than two decades, I was quite used to leading from the front, as many CEOs do. We know we have to set the vision, establish values, set strategy, build a team and achieve results. Like many of the CEOs I grew up with, I was quite used to leading from the front.

So, shortly after I became chairman of the board of Liz Claiborne (now Kate Spade), it was a surprise to learn that leading from the front was not what was required, or even expected. Though I was chairman, I was a member like every other board member. I had some special duties: to set meeting agendas, organize committees, communicate with the CEO, make sure the company met all of its public company obligations and, of course, make sure it met financial expectations.

It was 2007, and the company needed to adjust its strategy and execution to contend with market realities. Department stores were consolidating, and apparel companies were getting their margins squeezed. After more than a decade of rapid acquisitions, Liz Claiborne had too many brands. They desperately needed to be streamlined. I pushed an agenda forward with a rapid timetable to completion.

Apparently, in my zeal to move forward quickly, I stepped on a few committee members' toes. I realized I was making a mistake. During a critical discussion, I decided to drop back and let other board members take the lead. It is important to get all opinions on the table and it is essential to know who will be most likely to lead.

To my delight, dropping back to lead from the middle produced a very solid and executable plan. This became my method of leading through some very difficult years that followed during the most acute global financial crisis since the Great Depression.

This also recalls a reasoning I read in the book *The Art of Possibility* by Ben Zander, conductor of the Boston Philharmonic Orchestra, and his wife, Rosamund Stone Zander. He reminds us all that a conductor plays no instrument, but needs to get every other member of the orchestra to play perfectly on tune and in tempo to make beautiful music.

KAY'S TAKEAWAYS

- Leaders tend to lead from out front; letting other stakeholders take the lead is a way to lead from the middle.
- When there are other capable leaders in the room, it is important to get all opinions on the table.
- Much as an orchestra conductor does, leading from the middle can produce an executable plan.

LAURA STRONG

How to keep urgent—but not important—tasks from taking over your day.

SETTING PRIORITIES. Discipline in execution. These are the two things almost all entrepreneurs struggle with, whether they're in the start-up phase or are leading relatively mature companies.

One of the graduates of a mentoring program I participate in recently returned to share the lessons that had been most helpful to her, both professionally and personally. What was at the top of the list? I should have been able to guess: setting priorities and discipline in execution. Here are a few ways to increase your success at both.

Write a mission/vision/guiding-light/whatever-you-want-to-call-it statement.
This statement will identify the goals that will help your company to succeed. It should cover what your company does, how your product or service is unique, and who you are selling to. Here's how to write a decent one:

- Write in plain English. You don't need to post it on your website or proclaim it from the mountain-tops. (And I doubt you need a consultant to write it for you.)
- Allow enough leeway for the business to grow and pivot, but not so much that the company is trying to be all things to all people.
- Get key staff involved to make sure you are all headed in the same direction.
- After testing your statement for a few weeks, use the final draft as a guideline for allocating resources.
- Remember: You wrote the mission statement. If you need to, you can change it.

Articulating your mission can help you mobilize resources and assets more effectively. Often, these statements force entrepreneurs to confront their time management skills—or lack thereof. When it comes to achieving success for the business, what is your most valuable skill set? Do you spend most of your time using those skills? Are you willing and able to surround yourself with people who complement your strengths?

Learn to predict the future and avoid distraction.
The time management matrix of urgent vs. important tasks (said to be based on a concept from a Stephen Covey book) has been the topic of a number of authors, including some who focus on entrepreneurs.

Here's how it breaks down:

- If something is important and urgent, accomplish it now.

- If something is urgent but not important, try to avoid it.
- If something is important but not urgent, plan for it and get it done.
- If something is neither important nor urgent, skip it. Why waste your time?

Obviously, you need to spend time on things that are important. Urgency does not in itself deserve your attention. Things that are urgent are time-sensitive by their nature—but that's it.

Less obviously:

- Important items are guaranteed to move from "Not Urgent" to "Urgent" if you don't make sufficient time for them.
- Urgent things often feel important, even if they are not.

When you know what to look for, you'll discover that distraction due to urgency is everywhere. The real devils here are the items that are not important but appear urgent, because time sensitivity is easily mistaken for importance.

By knowing your mission, positioning your resources accordingly, and learning to recognize those things that truly require your attention, you can keep the "urgents" from taking over your day.

- Know what you want to accomplish and align your human capital and resources toward meeting that goal.
- Learn how to differentiate between what is urgent and important from what is urgent and not important. Prioritize accordingly.
- It's best to schedule time and plan to accomplish your important but not urgent tasks so they don't become important and urgent.

GET MORE TIME TO THINK: FOUR TIPS

ALEXANNDRA ONTRA

When's the last time you gave yourself some time
for quality, focused, creative thinking? Start here.

WITHOUT A DOUBT, the explosion of the Internet and mobile technology has made business faster, more efficient and less expensive. That's the good news. The bad news is that all this speed and accessibility creates an awful lot of clutter, mental and otherwise.

When a client emails you with a request, the typical reaction is to stop what you are doing and respond. The problem with this is that our brains are not dual-core processors! It's been proven in study after study that we are incapable of truly multitasking. We must stop one task, even if it's only for a very short time, to pick up another.

Rather than making us more efficient, the constant interruption of emails, IMs and calls is pulling our mental and physical resources from bigger, more strategically important projects. As a result, we are constantly left with half-finished or barely started micro projects. We're constantly busy, but we're not devoting any time to quality, creative, focused thinking.

Unfortunately, our jobs require that we be accessible. We cannot ignore our client's or boss's request, and ultimately we expect the same speed of response from our underlings. So the challenge lies in balancing the two: think-time and real-time. Here a few tips that I use to help keep a focus on the big picture for my business, while remaining accessible.

Set accomplishments for the day.
Take ten minutes in the morning to consider your goals for the day. Ask yourself what you want to achieve. If you have a meeting, set your own mental goals/objectives and envision that outcome. If you have to make sales calls, do the same. Knowing what you want to accomplish allows you to create a realistic to-do list.

Identify tasks that are best completed offline.
Treat yourself to quality work time where you can focus and be creative: time away from email, away from IM and away from the phone. Block out the time on your calendar beforehand and let your colleagues know you will be busy.

Manage interruptions.
There is nothing wrong with politely saying, "wait."

Open-air offices may foster collaboration, but they also encourage colleagues to wander into your space to discuss things of varying importance. You can judge the severity of the issue and then act accordingly. But you shouldn't constantly stop what you are doing just because someone asks you to.

Take a break.
A brief, planned change in your environment can do wonders for your productivity. Stroll around the block. Get a coffee. It will help your mind and body to refresh, recalibrate and focus.

While we can't (and shouldn't wish to) slow down the progress of business technology, we certainly can slow ourselves down long enough to make some good decisions about how best to spend our days.

KAY'S TAKEAWAYS

- Technology is great, but, more than ever, we are bombarded with emails and other communications that require our attention. It can be challenging to have time to think about issues that require more of our brain than a simple reply.
- Manage your time for responding to emails; schedule "thinking" time and create goals early in the morning for what you want to accomplish that day.
- Prioritize the importance of what is in front of you with what really needs your attention and react accordingly.

LEADERSHIP REQUIRES MORE FEMININE ATTRIBUTES
KAY KOPLOVITZ

So Proves the Latest Global Leadership Study:
The Athena Doctrine

LEADERSHIP IN THE TWENTY-FIRST CENTURY requires more of the attributes held by women. Thanks to the herculean efforts of two highly regarded researchers, John Gerzema and Michael D'Antonio, we now know this to be a fact. The team interviewed sixty-four thousand people in thirteen countries, men and women alike. The results are undeniable. The female traits of collaboration, flexibility and nurturing are winning out in a world that is becoming increasingly more social, interdependent and transparent.

Why is this study in leadership called *The Athena Doctrine*? Athena was the Greek goddess whose strength as a warrior came from wisdom and fairness. These are two of the leadership attributes highly valued by people around the globe who participated in this extensive survey. The macho paradigm of the past—dominance, strength, assertiveness and decisiveness—is giving way to the more open, creative, communal and flexible traits found more frequently among women.

In an era where the world is flat, according to author Thomas Friedman, communication may be with people next door or around the globe. The next great idea, company, movement or invention is as likely to come from Alexandria, Egypt, as from Alexandria, Virginia. Communication skills have become so important in the world in which we live, and women excel in communicating and socializing ideas, and are more open to opinions and comfortable with the dialogue.

Athena Doctrine authors Gerzema and D'Antonio take pains to document their leadership survey findings, with many stories from around the globe that support them. Of course, there are differences among nations, but the trends are extremely clear.

Corporate leaders would do well to take the findings of *The Athena Doctrine* to heart. In companies today, with social media in rapid rise and communication among employees a given, leaders have to inspire the rank and file and accept two-way communication as a skill they must possess. I believed when I led the USA Network (now USA Networks) and The Sci-Fi Channel (now SyFy) to prominence at the end of the '90s, that good ideas, critiques of company processes and understanding what works and doesn't work in the company could come from anyone at any level in the company. Maybe I was a bit ahead of my time, but now that I've read *The Athena Doctrine*, I realize that my leadership came more from my core beliefs, shared more by women than men. I was surprised by a comment made by my male COO that he thought I ran the company like a woman, and he was glad I did.

It was an open, collaborative, yet decisive era that drove our networks to the top of the competition.

This leads to the conclusions presented in *The Athena Doctrine*. The best leaders have a combination of traits held by women and men. That a combination of strength, decisiveness and authority when combined with flexibility, collaboration, creativity and openness, are the leadership qualities the best leaders for the twenty-first century will embody.

I agree.

KAY'S TAKEAWAYS

- People want leaders who are important, respectful, collaborative, trustworthy, open and flexible— attributes they assign more to women than men.
- Strong, bold, decisive, authoritarian are attributes most often assigned to men.
- A combination of both attributes is often most productive in creating superior results.

FIVE WAYS YOU CAN PROMOTE WOMEN'S LEADERSHIP

KELLY FITZSIMMONS

*You don't have to sign a petition or lobby anyone.
Instead, try showing that you care.*

T HERE I WAS, hand stretching high into the air with a gesture that screamed, "Pick me! PICK ME!" Was this third grade? No. I was a CEO in my twenties attending a Harvard Business School program. I was the youngest in the room by twenty years and one of three women.

After that first day, a gentleman approached and asked me to grab some coffee. He was kind, funny and eventually got to his point. "Why not let some other people share their experiences?" he asked.

I would love to say that I was grateful for his mentorship. But truthfully, I was mortified. I ended up learning a good deal that week, particularly about my own need to look smart.

When reflecting back on this incident, I think about the other women in the room. Why didn't they intervene? They never made eye contact, let alone approached me. Instead of taking action to help me, they created distance.

To be clear, I understand and respect why those women looked away. I too worry about how other women's actions will reflect on me. With so few of us at the table, the actions of one woman can be over-representative and reinforce ugly stereotypes.

So the question isn't whether or not we take action. We all take action—even in our silence. The question is whether or not we step in and help, even when our approach may be uncomfortable or even embarrassing.

And yet, if we want more successful women leaders, we need to step up to the challenge. And it is in that spirit that I have pulled together five things you can do today to help women succeed:

1. Step forward
If you are embarrassed by a coworker's action, arrange a private time to talk. In all likelihood, she's not clueless (like I was) about the misstep, and would welcome your support.

2. Ask questions
No one wants to be lectured. Ask simple, open-ended questions: "How do you feel after yesterday's presentation?" or, "What came up for you when you received the feedback?"

3. Listen
Once you ask a question, make room for the response. Staying silent is hard for me. I've found it helpful to silently repeat the mantra "I have no idea what she is going to say next." It keeps me curious and out of my head.

4. Be kind
It's easy to provoke shame accidentally. Use personal stories about your own mistakes to show your own humanness. "I remember this one time at my first board meeting, oh my…"

5. No advice, unless she literally begs you for it
I realize that this may sound contradictory, but any advice you are willing to share is for you, not the recipient. Your role is to show up and be supportive, not to dispense wisdom.

A leader is simply someone who is willing to take the first step. By having a willingness to step forward into the discomfort and make ourselves available to listen, we become leaders.

These actions may help your colleague as well—raising her up—but that is secondary. These steps are for you, first and foremost.

KAY'S TAKEAWAYS

- Being a leader to women can be as simple and as difficult as stepping in to help, especially when another woman behaves in a way we don't want to be associated with.
- There are too few women leaders, so we need to bring others along. Step forward with empathy and kindness, and share your own missteps.
- Resist the urge to dispense wisdom! No lectures or advice, just support. By taking this step, you become a leader and you lift yourself and your fellow women up.

HOW TO BE PREGNANT AND CEO: FIVE TIPS

BETTINA HEIN

*It's absolutely possible to be pregnant, or a new
mother, and a CEO at the same time. Some words
of wisdom from someone who's been there.*

ALL OF A SUDDEN, Marissa Mayer and I are about to have something very significant in common. At the age of thirty-seven, she is both the CEO of Yahoo and pregnant with her first child. I'm a year older, and the CEO of Pixability, a video marketing software company. Eighteen months ago, I gave birth to my daughter, Louisa. Here's what I've learned:

Don't believe what they say.
I've had investors, family and the general public wonder aloud whether I was being reckless to attempt both a baby and a post as CEO at the same time. But thanks to brain chemistry, having a baby is likely to improve your performance as CEO. Childbirth strengthens the area in your frontal cortex that governs executive function, important stuff such as planning, problem solving, verbal reasoning and multitasking. Hugely helpful.

Babies are simpler to manage than tech companies.
As an analytical person, I like to sink my teeth into hard problems.
A tech company is a pretty complex equation. Solving an equation for multiple variables while they change dynamically is what I do for a living. As it turns out, healthy babies have precious few variables: food, sleep, diaper, boredom and that's about it. You'll figure it out pretty quickly.

Don't take less than six weeks off.
I'm a hardcore workaholic. I was convinced that I'd be back in the office a few days after Louisa's birth. I simply couldn't do it. There's a reason most European countries have a legal ban on women working for six weeks after childbirth. Your brain may be ready to get back to work, but your body needs time to shrink your uterus and get back into fighting form. It just takes time. That said, I did give my first public speech three weeks after Louisa was born.

Take the baby to the office.
After six weeks at home, I felt like I was in baby prison. I was really anxious to get back to my team, so I started taking Louisa to work. This was a really positive experience. For the first year of her life, Louisa came to the office every day at lunch so I could nurse her. I started telling people: It takes not a village, but a tech company, to raise a child.

Keep your priorities straight.
This is the hardest part. As CEO, you have to keep your focus on what's important. Society tells you to prioritize your baby above all. People are depending on you for their livelihoods. So who wins? Some days, I've left the house in tears because

Louisa holds out her little arms, reaches for me and screams like I'm never coming back. But I had to make a meeting. On other days, I've canceled an important investor or customer meeting because I had been up all night with her. My advice is to step back regularly and see if, in the grander scheme of things, you are being true to both roles. If you're able to do this, the math will work out for both sides in the long run.

KAY'S TAKEAWAYS

- How women's amazing chemistry affects our brains makes it absolutely possible to do a good job while being pregnant or a new mother.
- Give your body at least six weeks to physically recover before going back to work full time.
- Prioritize and be creative. You may have to miss a meeting once in a while or bring baby to work for a period of time in order to stay true to both sides.

THREE: THE VALUE OF HUMAN CAPITAL

OVER THE FOURTEEN YEARS since we launched Springboard Enterprises to help women entrepreneurs raise venture capital, we've learned a very valuable lesson: Human capital is what leads to financial capital. This is the reason we emphasize the value of human capital in every boot camp and every coaching session we hold.

People don't easily recognize the value of human capital. Some even ask what it is. Human capital is the expertise and connections every person can bring to the table. For entrepreneurs, that can be in the form of advisors, mentors, connectors—members of the community who can help you advance your business.

One very stark example of human capital sourced from our network came to entrepreneur Joan Fallon, founder and CEO of Curemark, a company with a treatment for autism. Joan had developed a rather unorthodox method of treating the symptoms of autism using a digestible product. The problem was that Joan, a pediatric chiropractor, didn't have the right credentials or the research background to get the product through the labyrinth of the FDA.

In stepped one of Springboard's alums, board member Lauren Flanagan, who brought in Stacy Grant, an investment advisor at Morgan Stanley in San Francisco. Stacy introduced Joan to a client of hers who had fast-tracked drugs through the

FDA process. The result was that Curemark was able to get its drug through the FDA in three short years, practically unheard of. How did they do it? They combined it with another product that had already received FDA approval. That's human capital at work, providing remarkable results. The success of this process has led to continuous financial infusion into Curemark.

In a number of articles in Chapter Three, "The Value of Human Capital," you can learn how different entrepreneurs have utilized the value others bring to the table. I talk about finding the right mentor. Jules Pieri offers sage advice in "How to Get the Most out of Your Advisors." The important connection between academia and innovation is promoted in "Brainiacs for Your Business" by Sharon Flank, who shows how human capital can be turned into business opportunities.

I learned the real value of mining the customer's human values from a former business partner, Blake Mycoskie, the founder and CEO of Toms. He started with a simple idea of giving away one pair of shoes to children in need for every pair bought. The message appealed to customers of stores as widely ranging as Nordstrom's and Harry's Shoes, a local store on Manhattan's Upper West Side. The business generates more than $500 million in sales today. Lynley Sides, in "How to Make Social Responsibility Work for Your Company," explains how social responsibility and the human connection can work for your company.

Remember, human capital leads to financial capital. Mine your human capital connections before you need financial capital—you'll be glad you did.

HOW DO I FIND THE RIGHT MENTOR?

KAY KOPLOVITZ

The right mentor will be one of the most valuable resources you'll have in your whole career.

O NE OF THE MOST frequent questions I get from women in corporate positions and from entrepreneurs alike is how to find the right mentor. We have seen a rise of discussion about mentorship in business circles of all kinds in recent years. Yet it seems that finding the right one is still challenging to many.

It's easy to understand why. Not all people with experience necessarily make good mentors. It takes a certain emotional intelligence (EQ) to be a valuable mentor. Conversely, all people seeking mentors do not often know what they hope to gain from a mentor.

Let's start with what I would consider the most important factor in establishing a productive mentor/mentee connection. First, one has to establish a relationship. This should be someone you admire in your company or in your industry with whom you already have some communication and familiarity. If you don't have that, it is important to look for ways to bridge the gap. You can do this by offering up your assistance on a project, a task force or industry-wide initiative, or by participating in a common interest, for example on a health issue, a hobby or a community event. There are numerous ways to get to know people and one has to use imagination in order to make those connections.

Once a relationship is established, think through what it is you are seeking from a mentor. Remember, people in a position to give you guidance are likely to be very busy. Therefore, they will be making a decision as to whether or not they want to spend their time helping you. You will advance your request if you make clear what it is you are seeking advice about. Rather than being vague and general in making a request of someone, if you are clear about the advice you are seeking, you have a much better chance of getting a positive reply.

Once a mentor is secured, be very mindful of using your mentor's time wisely. You might find that there are ways to exchange values, providing the mentor with information on something of interest to them. Creating this two-way street is the best way to develop a long-term relationship. It will provide the best opportunity to turn a mentor into a sponsor, someone who has an interest in seeing you advance your career.

KAY'S TAKEAWAYS

- Identify people in the industry you admire.
- Be ready to offer service in exchange for mentorship.
- Read up on regulations in the industry.

HOW TO GET THE MOST OUT OF YOUR ADVISORS

JULES PIERI

It took ages to convince the right people to sit on your advisory board. So why aren't they helping?

As a CEO, you sign a high-pressure contract with your customers, investors and employees to solemnly swear to be faster, better, smarter than the next guy or gal. Unless you possess superpowers, it's impossible. You can't do this all on your own.

So imagine your company as a bunch of auto parts. As CEO, you hope to soon be at the wheel of a lean, mean driving machine. You don't personally need to know how to assemble the seats, the engine and the tires. But you do need to find people who can put the parts together so you can get on the road, fast. This is where advisors come in handy.

Here are three rules for putting together an advisory board that will get—and keep—you in gear:

- *Keep the load light.* Keep the number of active advisors in your company between three and six. Why? It's basic human psychology. Did you ever get an email asking for help, and then notice it that it was sent to fifteen people? Most people don't respond to such things, because they assume that one of the other fourteen people answered. The same is true of advisors. They need to feel needed before they'll extend themselves.

- *Don't be afraid to drop advisors along the way.* The skills you need from your advisors in the first years of your company will be radically different than what you need later on. Veteran advisors understand this. Manage expectations by using a formal agreement with equity compensation reviewed annually. Specify the expected time commitment and grant equity that assumes a year's involvement. In an early-stage company, one year's involvement will be worth somewhere between one-quarter and 1 percent of the equity in the company.
- *Do a lot of test-driving before putting people on the road with you.* What can seem like a burning need right now might be a distant memory six months later. Conversely, an advisor can be extremely enthusiastic for two months and then fade away, thanks to other demands and pressures in their life. You are looking for advisors who can consistently and quickly answer your calls, and who have enough depth and coverage to merit a seat in the car.

In addition to forming a great advisory board, consider joining a community of peer advisors. You'll get immediate help, you may find candidates for your advisory board, and you'll practice the art of giving and taking advice, which will benefit you in multiple ways.

To find great peers, I've had good luck with the Creative Good Councils, a peer network of digital executives across a wide range of industries and geographies. They've announced a free membership for qualified candidates. I've been a member for several years and it's been very helpful. Because there is careful vetting of applications to ensure that only senior-level talent is admitted, the quality of participants is high.

Just as driving from coast to coast is an intense and exhilarating process, with unexpected weather, boring interludes and breathtaking scenery, so goes the journey of building a business. You wouldn't invite just anyone along on that road trip, but it sure would be lonely doing it alone. Find some trusted advisors to take along for the ride.

KAY'S TAKEAWAYS

- Leaders of companies need a sounding board of advisors who have diverse talents to help them "steer the ship."
- Keep the number of advisors just right (three to six) and formalize agreements about their pay or equity and what the time commitment you require in return. Create one-year term agreements and review annually so you can rotate the advisor to suit your changing needs or end the agreement if it's not working out.
- Join a peer group of advisors with which you can practice giving and taking advice.

BRAINIACS FOR YOUR BUSINESS

SHARON FLANK

*Our company is stocked with scientists, but we still
can't solve every technical challenge ourselves.
Enter the scientific advisory board.*

M Y COMPANY, INFRATRAC, is science central. And we
still can't possibly overcome every technical challenge
we're faced with all on our own. The answer? A scientific advisory board. Scientific advisors aren't easy to recruit, but they add
invaluable brainpower to your company. Getting them on board
is an art as well as a science.

Using instruments small enough to fit in a smartphone, we
use light to analyze the components of drugs, allowing us to
detect counterfeits. While we were in the development phase,
our challenge was to learn about portability technologies and
then turn that knowledge into marketable applications in multiple industries. We knew that melding the applications and the
science would require some serious expertise, so we sought out
the smartest people we could find and started peppering them
with questions. Then we asked the best contributors to join a
scientific advisory board. Here's what we learned in the process
of getting them to sign on.

Before you think about putting together a compensation package, you need to realize that most of the people who will make great scientific advisors are not businesspeople. Their priorities and values may not be the same as yours. Money is generally not a key motivator. We found that it was worth asking them the big questions: What is important to you? Do you want to get rich? Do you want to keep your day job? Do you want us to provide opportunities for your students? It is not likely that a professor will give up tenure to join your company. That's partly because of the job security. It's also partly because professors get to choose their research topics, and employees don't.

What, then, do scientists and academics tend to value?

- *Publication,* especially academic articles that further their careers. You can help by providing questions and data worth studying and even by helping to write the article and getting it submitted to a journal. Promoting your advisors as conference speakers, even at poster sessions, is a good way to raise their visibility—and yours. Presenters often attend conferences for free, which is a good thing for your budget. Their presence also attracts other experts, which can be a great recruitment strategy.
- *Patents.* In a perfect world, the advisors would come up with the ideas, and all you'd have to do is pay the lawyers.
- *Ideas.* Put the smart people together, by email if necessary, give them a hard problem to gnaw on, and let them learn from other members of your advisory board. This is the fun part—a frolic in the park for

an active mind. Do the prep work: Make sure everyone knows the existing state of the art, including recent patent filings, so you don't waste time reinventing the wheel.

- *Influence.* Academics' ivory-tower ideas don't always make real things happen. You can help fix this problem, which can be extremely rewarding. An advisor may have an advanced technology in search of practical applications and real-world tests. You can provide those applications and tests, then flip this back into a scholarly paper of the type: "Use of [Academic Technique] to [Solve Your Real-World Problem]." These serve a dual purpose: The advisors get a publication, and show that they are doing something important. You get a white paper that serves as validation.

- *Bragging rights.* You can sometimes make your advisors happy just by showcasing them on your website, in your blog, and even in a press release. The press release works particularly well for retired experts: They can hardly issue a release about themselves, but it shows they are doing active, exciting things that matter.

- *Equity.* You are going to make it big, and your advisors deserve to share in your success. Some of this is about long-term financial rewards, of course, but there are bragging rights to consider, too: They were smart enough to see the wisdom of your vision.

As one of our advisors put it, "You can't afford to pay me what I'm worth—and anyway, this is what I do for fun." What fun: Our advisors have given us hundreds of hours of free labor, multiple patents and credibility.

KAY'S TAKEAWAYS

- To attract scientists to your advisory board, offer them something of value in exchange for their expertise.
- Ideas for what you can offer: Publication, patents, equity, bragging rights.

THREE WAYS TO EXPAND YOUR FUTURE

DENISE BROSSEAU

By connecting with people who face hurdles similar to yours, you can vastly expand the possibilities for your own future.

B OOKS ABOUT INNOVATION fascinate me, because they help me understand how people come up with new, world-changing ideas. At the top of my pile is Steven Johnson's *Where Good Ideas Come From*. In it, he talks about the "adjacent possible"—a sort of shadow future that is just at the edge of today's present and offers immense potential.

Think of it like this: You are standing in a room with four doors. You open and walk through each door, and on the other side is another room with three more doors. As you open door after door, entering room after room, you will soon find yourself in a room that you did not have access to from the room where you started.

That's your adjacent possible. You can't see it today. You can't get to it today, at least not directly. But you can get there. The reward for doing so is access, not only to a wealth of new ideas, resources, expertise and opportunities you would have never known were available, but also to a world of people who are eager to learn from your experiences and teach you about things you know nothing about.

The most successful executives and entrepreneurs I know understand this model. So when I work with my clients, I push them to think about and explore how they can open lots of doors and tap into their adjacent possible as often and as broadly as they can.

How can you do that? Here are three steps everyone can take:

- Begin by convening and collaborating with those people within your own organization who are tackling other parts of the same challenge that you are. Identify like-minded individuals and invite them to lunch or organize a call to explore the idea of knowledge-sharing on a regular basis.
- Build your personal network by identifying others outside your company who share the same job title as yours or who are facing a similar next hurdle in their company or their career progression. LinkedIn is a great tool for this. Ask for a call, meeting, or get-together at an upcoming trade show or industry event. Build a connection and agree to collaborate or share ideas whenever possible.
- If you are tackling a big challenge (clean water, global poverty, technological advancement), convene those in your industry, including those at competitive organizations. Set a simple agenda of sharing what your organization is learning and ask others to do the same. This sort of co-opetition model will help everyone expand their adjacent

possible and create a more robust set of solutions for the entire industry.

No matter what issue, challenge, project or initiative you are working on, you are not alone. There are always others in your wider ecosystem if you begin to open the door to those possibilities. But you need to open the first door.

What will you do this year to connect with those in your ecosystem and broaden your own adjacent possible?

KAY'S TAKEAWAYS

- Your "adjacent possible" future is something you can't see today. You can't even get there today, but you can get there. This is where innovation lives. Learn how to open the doors to this future.
- Regularly exchange knowledge with people in your organization, industry peers and—if it's a big enough idea—competitive organizations so that everyone can expand their adjacent possible.
- Cast a wide net into your ecosystem and begin to open the doors that will eventually lead you to the adjacent possible future you are creating.

HOW TO MAKE SOCIAL RESPONSIBILITY
WORK FOR YOUR COMPANY

LYNLEY SIDES

As customer attitudes change, "giving back" is no longer an option. It's a necessity. Here's how to make it good business, too.

W HEN I WAS on my first start-up, social responsibility was still the concern of a small tree-hugging minority. But today phrases such as "profits with purpose" and "conscious capitalism" are topping prediction and trend lists.

Most executives are aware of global social issues and want to make a difference. Here's why that's harder than it sounds:

- Expectations for businesses to operate responsibly are at their highest point in history.
- Public satisfaction with the social impact of Corporate America is lower than ever.
- In tough times, doing good becomes unsustainable if it doesn't support the bottom line.

So how can your growing company do good in ways that are also good for business? Here's how to start:

1. Tie your brand to your social mission as early as possible.
Start now. Create a brand that makes people feel good about
affiliating with it.

- Cause-conscious consumers and employees see
  themselves as investing in you, not just exchanging
  money for products or time for a paycheck.
- The value your customers attribute to your products
  extends beyond tangible factors like function, dura-
  bility and quantity.
- If buying your product makes customers feel good
  and enhances their identity, you'll be able to command a price that includes that value. You'll also set
  the bar higher for your competitors.

Growing companies across all industries, such as Method,
Annie's Homegrown, YesTo, Toms Shoes and Warby Parker,
are setting new standards for sustainable operations, corporate
giving and smart branding. In doing so, they're forcing big-brand
competitors to spend time and money rethinking their value
propositions and marketing strategies.

In a great example of corporate conversion, Hershey's
recently committed to sourcing only certified cocoa for one
of its product lines. Yes, it took months of pressure and a lot of
negative PR, but Hershey's is now benefiting from the switch.
In a sense, they didn't have much choice: Smaller fair trade
chocolate companies like sweetriot present alternatives that
feel better to consumers and can make tangible dents in the
big brands' numbers.

2. Spread the word.

There are lots of ways to give back. You can:

- Operate sustainably.
- Treat people well.
- Make environmentally friendly products.
- Give to worthy causes.

No matter how you integrate social responsibility into your business, it's important that you let people know right away. The earlier you communicate social responsibility as an important part of your value proposition, the better job they will do at differentiating your company, and the more value you will build as a result. If you put off being a good citizen until you think you can afford it, your customers will have already formed beliefs about your brand. Changing those perceptions is difficult and expensive.

3. Make your customers your partners.

Perhaps the easiest way for most growing companies to be socially responsible is through giving. And if it's done right, giving can do more than help good causes and create goodwill. It can drive real value for your business.

- Consumers are nearly twice as likely to buy or recommend a product if it's affiliated with a cause they care about.
- Simply writing a check to a charity and advertising that you did it doesn't engage consumers or inspire them to tell anyone about it.

- If a company's giving isn't integrated with business activities, it doesn't directly boost the bottom line.

To create more value for their brands, Coke, Project RED and Starbucks have built interactive web experiences around their giving, working with their customers to make a positive impact. Pepsi and Chase let customers vote on the companies' corporate giving, engaging them socially. Why not take it one leap forward? Drive greater business value by allowing consumers to choose where the cause dollars go and then directly drive purchases as a part of the process. Today's consumers expect to be empowered and engaged socially. And when they're empowered and engaged by your brand, they will purchase and become advocates for it, sending their friends and colleagues to buy from you too.

That's a win for social good and a win for your business.

- Tie your company to social mission as early as possible.
- Giving back makes good business sense. However, it can prove difficult to maintain long term while trying to make a profit.
- Social mission must be embedded in all corporate messaging.
- Engage your customers in the mission.
- Since giving back is the new norm, have your company connected to a social mission from the start, so your customers and employees will feel good about their relationship to your brand.
- Connecting the consumer and employees to a cause creates a strong emotional bond, which will keep them engaged with your products and sharing with their friends.

STILETTO NETWORK: THE EMERGING POWER
OF WOMEN'S HUMAN CAPITAL

KAY KOPLOVITZ

> *Women are changing the rules of the game in*
> *business and creating powerful new networks.*

YOU CAN REALLY CAPTURE the emerging power being wielded by women using their human capital networks in the world of business and power in Pamela Ryckman's book, *Stiletto Network: Inside the Women's Power Circles That Are Changing the Face of Business*. It came "on the heels" (pun intended) of two other powerful books that came out in spring 2013, *Lean In* by Sheryl Sandberg and *The Athena Doctrine* by John Gerzema and Michael D'Antonio. Each of them captures the changing world of women, business and power from different perspectives. But if you want to know how this is being done, *Stiletto Network* is the one that can inform you.

Pamela started out on the road to her research to fill a personal need. She has written for the *New York Times*, the *Financial Times, Fortune, CNNMoney*, the *Observer* and many more. But when she took a break to raise her children, she found on her return that she had lost her footing.

Then she attended a women's conference in California and an amazing pattern started to unfold. She met woman after woman who introduced her to others, and Pamela started to realize that the landscape was shifting. Not only were women not balking at helping each other achieve their goals, they were promoting their friends, business associates and colleagues. The women were active, confident and collaborative, and intuitively knew who Pamela needed to know next. The electronic Rolodexes came out, and one connection after another was made. This is the power of women using their human capital network to effect change. This is the heart of the Stiletto Network: friendly, open, selfless and stylish women who opened up with their stories.

What has resulted is a beautiful mosaic of how women are changing the rules of business to suit themselves and their lifestyles. At last, we are learning to earn power and use power for ourselves and others.

The power of the human capital network emerges in the story of Shauna Mei, who started her career at Goldman Sachs and left after only a couple years to join a Goldman client and start a research firm in luxury goods. That led to her becoming the COO for a client company and having her AHA moment, which is when she left that company to start her own online luxury lifestyle company, AHAlife. That is when she returned to her Goldman contact Janet Hanson, founder of 85 Broads (85broads.com), the global professional women's network. She discussed her plans for AHAlife and her need for capital. One discussion led to another until Shauna wound up raising her angel capital primarily from the group of 85 Broads members. The human capital network effect was definitely in place.

Stories like Shauna's fill the book. Über-connectors Kim Moses, Heidi Roizen, Maggie Wilderotter, Heidi Messer, Ann Winblad, Gerry Laybourne, Alexa von Tobel and dozens and dozens more provide the blueprint for how these Stiletto Networks are formed, operate and provide real value to their members.

Time after time, you learn that the characteristics women hold and cherish are becoming more the norm for business today. Attributes such as collaboration, diversity, judgment, intuition, partnership, listening, inclusiveness, flexibility, selflessness and loyalty mean a lot.

Interestingly, these are the attributes that are documented in the extensive global research done by John Gerzema and Michael D'Antonio in *The Athena Doctrine*. They tested the gender associations of one hundred twenty-five attributes among sixty-four thousand men and women and came up with some pretty conclusive results. The business world is decisively moving toward leadership in the attributes most commonly described as feminine.

One might expect that the attributes more characteristic of men would be going out of fashion, but neither *The Athena Doctrine* nor *Stiletto Network* takes that position. Male attributes of decisiveness, authority, power, ambition, aggressiveness and the like have their place too. It's the combination of both gender attributes that will be required for leadership as we move forward.

What author Ryckman is attempting to do is to give women a road map of how they can form their own Stiletto Networks and help others as well as themselves succeed in business, and indeed in life. That road map relies in part on being able to harness the power of our human capital networks.

I find that the stories told in her book reflect what I see changing every day in the world of entrepreneurs, where I spend a good portion of my time working with women entrepreneurs who are participating in the Springboard Enterprises network to raise capital. What they learn on their way to raising capital is that it is that the human capital, the human network, that leads you to success. That's the story of the Stiletto Network, told in the rich stories of the women brave enough to tell them.

KAY'S TAKEAWAYS

- Women are using their attributes of openness, collaboration, inclusiveness, transparency and trustworthiness to help their colleagues achieve success. This is a cultural change from earlier generations.
- Women are changing the rules of how business is being conducted to better reflect their strengths. This is documented in recent research, which cites feminine attributes as the most desirable for leadership in the twenty-first century.

FOUR: RAISING CAPITAL

A FUNDAMENTAL QUESTION I am often asked by entrepreneurs is: When is the right time to raise capital? It's not always easy to answer that without marketplace metrics to measure your chances. Frankly, many people have no idea when and how to start. Even savvy serial entrepreneurs ponder this question, so don't feel you're alone.

Having a little historical perspective might help to understand the market.

When we first launched Springboard in 2000, entrepreneurs were raising unbelievable amounts of money from angels, and Series A first-round institutional funding was averaging $8 million to $15 million. Those were the heady days of Internet 1.0, and venture capitalists were pouring money over the transom. You had to drink from a fire hose to take in the cash that VCs were throwing around.

But times have changed. Technology has made it cheaper, faster and easier to launch a business today. In recent years, Software as a Service (SAAS) such as SalesForce.com; cloud computing, offered by big platforms such as Amazon; mobility in the form of iPads and tablets; and 3-D printing in manufacturing and social media have made it easier to start a business, at often one-tenth the cost of what it was a decade ago. Beginning in 2013, it became possible to raise funds from accredited investors via crowdfunding, adding a whole new route to capital to the entrepreneurs' choices.

So entering a business is easier, which in turn creates more competition. Marketing becomes more ubiquitous, yet more competitive. Establishing a brand is more challenging.

What to do?

Find clear advice in Carol Politi's article, "Are You Ready to Raise Money? How to Tell." In it, she offers specific guidelines to help you with that decision. "Six Steps to a Perfect Pitch," by Renee Lorton, will help you understand the value of telling a good story.

There is a great deal to learn about the process of raising capital. One important step is identifying potential investors. You need to know as much about them as possible before meeting with them. Ellie Cachette offers some very good advice in her article "Finding the Right Investor."

Entrepreneurs can learn a great deal from industry experts, from the investor comments during pitches and even from tracking competitors. Often, company target markets or revenue models need to make a significant correction. This is called a pivot, and you can learn more about knowing when to pivot from Leslie Bane in her article, "Is It Time to Pivot? How to Tell."

Of course, there are many other decisions one has to make about raising capital, among them understanding the terms of the capital one is taking on, whether it is debt or equity, the terms sought by the lender or investor, and whether this is good for you. There are many online sources for these documents, including the Springboard website (sb.co) and the Angel Capital Association (aca.org).

Be sure to check out local sources, too, as capital could come from a variety of sources. You can find out about local angel investing groups on the Angel Capital Association site. There are a plethora of online lending and investing platforms, connecting companies to sources of capital.

Sometimes, raising capital is not the right decision for your company. Today, many corporations have their own strategic investing units and these, too, scour the landscape for early- and late-stage companies to buy. Sharon Kan explains her decision to sell as an early-stage company in her article, "When It Makes Sense to Sell Your Company Early."

Raising capital in the public market through crowdfunding became a reality on September 23, 2013, when the Securities and Exchange Commission issued rules for soliciting accredited investors in public under Title II of the JOBS Act. This new access to capital is one way entrepreneurs are raising funds, and you can find out more about the types of crowdfunding available in Luan Cox's article, "Crowdfunding (and Crowdfinance) 101." You can also learn the best practices for crowdfunding from Chance Barnett in his article, "Seven Crowdfunding Tips Proven to Raise Funding."

Knowing where to source capital is very important, and especially true for women founders. Joshua Henderson makes the process of finding good sources easier in his article, "The Ultimate Guide to Finding Women Investors."

First, you really need to know if you are ready to raise outside capital. The experiences of those who have done so in this chapter will give you insight for this decision.

*Getting outside money will dramatically change the
way you run your company. Are you ready for that?*

MANY ENTREPRENEURS VIEW raising outside angel
or venture investment as a baseline requirement for
starting their business—before they even write a line of code
or bring a customer on board. An idea, a big scalable market
target, a set of PowerPoint slides and you are ready to go.

This has predictable consequences: You get told that the
company isn't ready or that the market is too difficult. If you
can make a great pitch, you may end up making a ninety-degree
turn or going after an adjacent market rather than executing
the business plan you had in mind.

The alternative: Run as lean as you can and raise as little
money as possible while you work to prove that your business
model and product work. Doing the basic work of testing and
tweaking your business model becomes a whole lot more difficult when you are sitting on funds that are supposed to be used
to make that same business model come to life.

Here are a few questions to ask yourself to determine
whether you should try to raise money:

1. Do you have customers, and do they like your product?
Have your target customers tried your product, and how much do they like it? Will they (or customers like them) buy more? If not, can you get to the point where you do have paying, satisfied customers without going to experienced angel or venture investors? Most investors do not want to invest in science experiments. They want to see some kind of evidence that you've got a real business in the making.

2. Are you ready to execute, or are you still learning?
Most investors will be focused on measuring how well you execute on your business plan. They aren't particularly impressed by watching you innovate and brainstorm your way toward a business plan. Once you take money, you will need to execute, execute, execute. In the early stage of a company, this can limit much-needed experimentation.

3. Are you ready to raise more capital in one to two years?
Your early investors are probably not funding you to profitability. They are funding you to reach specific milestones, and after you reach them, you'll need to go out and raise more money. So what are your milestones? Are they well-defined? Can you meet them comfortably?

4. Can you take advantage of investor involvement on your board?
Investors will contribute to your business plan and help drive corporate strategy—from their vantage point as investors. They will naturally endorse execution and sales-oriented plans in order to drive a better return on their investment.

If you say no to the majority of these questions, you're not ready to raise money. Avoid that distraction, and keep your head down until you've made more progress. Certainly, you'll want to get feedback from friendly advisors, but don't expect to raise start-up capital from experienced investors until you have sorted out your value proposition, tested and validated it with customers, and are ready to define and meet established business-plan goals.

Remember, there are other choices. Bootstrapping is increasingly preferred for many early-stage companies. "Lean" start-up approaches are popular for a reason. Just as agile software development is driving more effective development, agile business processes allow you to efficiently hone your business plan. Test and iterate until you get it right, while spending as little as you can.

Most bootstrapped investors are also going to end up tapping some amount of personal savings or friends and family investment. Putting your own money—and that of your friends or family—to work is a focusing event in itself.

- Taking on investor funds changes your business. Before taking in investors, wisely consider whether or not your business is ready for it.

- Ask yourself if your business has met customer and sales milestones, is progressing at a rate that will require cash again within a year, and if you are ready to execute your business plan.

- If your assessment indicates you are not at the point of taking in investor money, focus on testing and validating your model while spending as little as you can.

SIX STEPS TO A PERFECT PITCH

RENEE LORTON

You'd be surprised at the difference a perfect pitch can make. But first you have to get there.

NO MATTER HOW OBVIOUS it may seem that you have a winning idea, the ultimate success of your company is entirely dependent on how well you can personally drum up interest, excitement and investment.

Which means you need to pitch. A lot.

Ironically, the ultimate goal in developing your pitch is to make it seem as if you are not pitching at all. Your audience should feel as if they are taking part in a very interesting conversation, and should be left wanting more.

With more than twenty years' experience creating and delivering hundreds, if not thousands, of pitches for customers, analysts and investors, I've developed a step-by-step methodology to getting your pitch nailed.

The six steps:

1. Take inventory and take heart.
You likely have a great foundation for your pitch in materials you have already created. Pull together every presentation, product description, scribble, customer praise (or lashing) that you've

ever seen. Dedicate one to two days with your team to sort through, filter and organize it. Be prepared to investigate the gaps you'll uncover and take a new look at the competition. It's best to do this off-site with a barrel of junk food and have some fun with it.

2. Take your position.

Before you construct a pitch, it's critical that you apply both creative thinking and discipline around your positioning and messaging. If you don't have a knack for marketing, this is a great time to invest in a pro who can facilitate this process. You will need to decide on an overall message and, at most, two to three supporting points. Your positioning and messaging is just as fundamental to your ultimate success as any "secret sauce" or competitive advantage. A compelling, sticky message is make-or-break for any venture.

3. Choose amongst your children.

Once you've decided on your key message and positioning, do the math and put your deck together. Count on one or two minutes per slide, and ruthlessly limit the number of slides.

You will probably need to develop a number of versions of your pitch, depending on how much time you have. For a one-hour customer or investor presentation, a good guideline is to kick off with a fifteen- to twenty-minute pitch (that means ten to fifteen slides, max), plus a two- to five-minute demo (live, video or slide). Leave at least a third of the meeting for introductions, follow-up and next steps. The only excuse for running out of time is because you had great audience questions, not because you couldn't edit yourself.

4. Get your razzle-dazzle on.

Script every word and time your delivery. And I mean every word. Be sure you are doing the talking and not hoping the slide will do it for you. It's death to your presentation to have your audience reading lengthy slides while you're talking. Bullet points should be five words or less. No more than five bullet points per page.

Once you have timed your script to one to two minutes per slide, you should reduce the script to the bare minimum. What you want is a CliffsNotes version of your presentation— enough to prompt you, but not enough to tempt you to read your notes, word for word, if the jitters hit. Practice out loud, on video, in the mirror, with your team—no fewer than ten times. You should be able to deliver the pitch without having to look at the slides.

As you practice, you'll gain confidence with your message. Think of your practice sessions as stage rehearsals at a theater production. Just like stage actors, you will need to bring the identical enthusiasm, emotion, emphasis and storytelling every day, and sometimes ten times in a day. So pull out those tap shoes and top hat and get in character. This is your big show!

5. Gather your friendlies and give it a go.

You need at least three practice sessions, and you need solid feedback at each.

"Friendlies" are not the same as cheerleaders. Friendlies need to be ruthless, and you must encourage them to not hold back. Over time, you'll learn that the worst outcome from an investor or customer pitch is silence and a polite, "Thank you, and best of luck." Listen to your critics and buy them lunch for beating you up.

6. Stick a fork in it.

At some point you need to declare it done and go for it. Creating your pitch, and getting it ready for prime time, is probably going to take you three to ten weeks. You don't do this in a day. Once you begin delivering your pitch, it will evolve as you learn the positives and failing points and make tweaks and adjustments. Once you have your pitch nailed, you will be amazed at how foundational it is to your venture. Pitching your venture should feel as natural as breathing. With the right pitch, whether you are in a conference hall with a thousand people or having a glass of wine at a networking event, whether it is a structured presentation or an elevator pitch, your messages, supporting points and, most important, your enthusiasm, will all weave together naturally to prompt excitement and action from your audience.

KAY'S TAKEAWAYS

- Engage in the act of storytelling.
- Write out your entire pitch, then reduce it to simplest form for different lengths: two-, five- and ten-minute scenarios.
- Practice before your friends. Ask for honest and direct feedback.

ELLIE CACHETTE

Before writing a check, an investor is going to know every last thing about you. Here's how to return the favor.

ONCE YOU'VE GOT INVESTORS invested in your company, your first reaction may be to break out the champagne. But be careful. Just as investors do due diligence on you and your company, you should be doing due diligence on them. Here's how:

Instinct and chemistry
Do you like the investor? Can you communicate well virtually? While there is a lot of emphasis on face-to-face relationships, the truth is that once your start-up takes off, the odds of you and your investor ever being in the same city at the same time are very slim. If communicating via email is tricky in the early days, watch out. It's only likely to get more difficult over time.

Crunchbase
Go to crunchbase.com and make it your friend. Crunchbase lets you find out all sorts of details about your potential investor and the investor's fund. AngelList is fine, but to me, Crunchbase is

more relevant. It's more sterile, less social, just the facts. Here's what you're looking for:

- An investor's personal investments
- Current or previous funds
- Investments made within a current or previous fund. What types of company does this person invest in, and at which stage?
- Founders that have accepted money from this investor. Get in contact with them. Grill them.
- Between Crunchbase and your own network, see if you can find an entrepreneur that turned down an investment from your potential financier, or one that had a round fall through. Often you learn more about investors from the deals they don't do than the ones that they fund.

Google
Many investors have spent years or even entire careers working behind the scenes, so Googling them may be less fruitful than you'd expect. Still, keep an eye out for:

- Old blog posts or rants about other investors or entrepreneurs
- Hobbies and personal interests
- Previous employers or funds that you may not be aware of

Facebook
Before an investor writes a check, they will want to know every single detail about you and your life. Do your best to return the

favor. See if they will be your Facebook friend or if they have a semi-open profile on Facebook. Transparency is always a good sign. If your potential investor is really loved, they may have reached the maximum number of Facebook friends (five thousand) and may be unable to add you to the list. This is always a good sign and probably someone you want to become close with, whether or not they invest.

Competing term sheets

A competing term sheet or letter of intent will help you get an idea of how good a deal your investor is offering. Of course, it isn't always possible to get a competing term sheet, but you might be able to get a friend or founder of a similar-sized company to share a term sheet with you. Make it clear that you don't mind if they scrub out names or confidential info.

It's important is to share investment documents with other founders. Some investors might pass on your company because they don't think they can get a good deal, or because they only invest with certain terms. It'll be a huge help to know what terms other companies are getting. Also bear in mind that "standard" terms can vary hugely by region—this is one time there is almost no such thing as too much research!

- Before you accept that check from your potential investor, do your due diligence on them and their company. Check the successes or failures of their previous investments.
- Follow your instincts and observe if their responsiveness and communication style suits you.
- Don't negotiate terms in a bubble. Share investment documents with other founders and get a competitive term sheet.

IS IT TIME TO PIVOT? HOW TO TELL
LESLIE BANE

"Pivots" come in all shapes, sizes and varieties.
How to see a course correction coming.

IN THE EARLY DAYS, an entrepreneur's success at raising money and recruiting strategic advisors depends mostly on a grand vision and a business plan that shows how everyone can make a lot of money. But what if that plan isn't working out as you hoped? What if you see a new opportunity that looks better? How can you tell if you should stay the course or abandon it?

To decide, you've first got to overcome two styles of working that can make it hard for you to do a good job of evaluating your own business and sizing up other options:

- *Head down.* It's easy to be so focused on getting to the next milestone that you fail to notice what the market or your competition is doing. This can mean that outside factors force you to make a change. Far better to identify the need for change upfront.
- *Idea love.* You are so in love with your idea that you try to do too much, too soon. You ignore the advice of people telling you not to bite off more than you can chew, probably because you don't fully

appreciate how much you can accomplish with a specific amount of money within a specific amount of time. In this case, you may need to change course because you run out of money.

How can entrepreneurs avoid these mistakes?

- *Make change a part of your company culture.* At first, I found it very difficult to accept and communicate change. I worried that those around me would lose confidence in my ability as a founder, leader and visionary. It took some time to realize that entrepreneurs are forced to make fundamental decisions relating to their product, solution, business model and pricing structure all the time. It's best for all involved if everyone gets used to this, fast.
- *Don't go it alone.* The beauty of running your own business is that you really do get to call the shots. Day-to-day, no one's telling you what to do. The flip side of this is that you need to lean on those around you for guidance, perspective and, yes, coaching. Just because you're the founder or CEO doesn't mean you can't or shouldn't take advice from a wide range of people—in fact, the opposite is true.
- *Leverage and listen.* Leverage your network, advisory board members and thought leaders in the space to help you challenge your assumptions on a regular basis. You can do this around the water cooler (if you have one) or you can conduct a more structured strengths, weaknesses, opportunities and threats analysis.

Course corrections happen all the time. The savvy investor understands that business plans change, business models need to be adjusted, and that knowing when to zig or zag is one of the hallmarks of a great entrepreneur.

KAY'S TAKEAWAYS

- In order to assess whether it is time to pivot your business model or not, you need to look outside your company at market forces and competitors.
- Change is a constant for entrepreneurs. Institute a culture of constant change and pivots will naturally flow from insights gained.
- Investors understand that business models evolve. Engage them in decisions to change course before approvals are required.

NOPE, YOUR INVESTORS CAN'T HELP

SUSAN ASKEW

With a boom in vc, it's tempting to start fund-raising. But can money really fix what ails your company?

T HANKS TO A THAW—some would say bubble—in venture capital investing, raising money no longer seems like such a crazy idea. The latest tech IPOs, with the Facebook offering still to come, have raised hopes for more successful exits. [Editor's note: Facebook's IPO came a month after this blog was posted.]

I've raised outside money for two businesses, once in the height of the Internet boom and once again after the bust. Before you get caught up in the idea of outside investment, take a step back and understand what that money—and the investors who come along with it—can and can't do for you.

What investment capital can do is fairly obvious. It can:

- *Jump-start expansion.* All of a sudden, you're no longer scraping by. Instead, there's now money for spending on lots of things: increased production capacity, opening new facilities nationally or internationally, making hires, etc.

- *Build your brand* through expenditures on advertising, social networking and publicity.
- *Expand your network* of contacts, increasing your visibility with potential partners, board members, advisors and others who can give you a boost.
- *Provide mentoring* and executive development (with the right investors).

Less well understood is what investment capital can't do for a business. A misunderstanding here can mean the difference between success and failure. So, consider for a moment that outside money can't:

- *Fix flaws in your business model.* If the market is saturated, the barriers to entry low, or the target audience too small, throwing money at the business won't change anything. Ask yourself, is it really the lack of money that is holding us back, or is there a weakness in the model that needs to be addressed?
- *Buy customers and revenue.* While capital can buy brand visibility, it cannot buy customers. You have to have a product/service that people are willing to pay for. You can give away the razors, but you have to sell the blades or the shaving gel... or something.
- *Create a path to profitability.* If your costs are greater than your revenue, you can't keep raising money to fill the gap. Remember the joke from the dot-com days? We're losing money but we're going to make

it up in volume? (Think Pets.com.) Eventually, you need to be profitable.

- *Guarantee success*, or even that the business will be around in a couple of years. You have to continue to innovate, provide a good product or have high switching costs. Otherwise customers will leave you for a competitor.

The bottom line is that fundamentals matter. Investors know that success depends on a solid plan, a lucrative target market, a good team, a product that solves a problem or fills a pressing need, competitive advantage and a path to profitability. Without the fundamentals, you cannot succeed. No amount of money will make these things magically appear, even if an investor is willing to invest in their absence.

With the fundamentals in place, the next consideration is scalability. Many successful businesses work because they are local. Scaling is either prohibitively expensive, or the trust of the community is so critical to the success of the business that the business just can't live outside the community. Money can't change that. That said, there are many businesses that can leverage economies of scale to create national or international businesses. Know which category you fit in.

Investment capital can benefit your business in many positive ways, but it is not a panacea. Understand what your business really needs—is it money or is it better fundamentals? The money follows the fundamentals, not the other way around.

- Before you look for an investor, understand what that money will and will not be able to do for your business.
- Investor money can help grow your business and contacts rapidly, and help you build your brand as well as provide mentoring.
- Investor money cannot buy customers or fix a flawed business plan that lacks solid fundamentals.

WHEN IT MAKES SENSE TO
SELL YOUR COMPANY EARLY

SHARON KAN

We idolize entrepreneurs, like Mark Zuckerberg,
who hung on when everyone urged them to sell.
But sometimes selling early makes a lot of sense.

I N 2007, I STARTED a company called Tikatok.com, an
online self-publishing platform for children. Just twenty-two
months later, I had the opportunity to sell my company to Barnes
& Noble, and was suddenly faced with a big decision. Do we
remain a start-up and keep building the business on our own, or
do we become part of a larger, established company right away?

I wasn't planning to sell my company this early. The opportunity just presented itself and after much thought, I decided
to take it.

Why did I say yes? I was well aware that a big part of entrepreneurship is indeed the exit. You either sell the company
after years and years of building it, or try for an IPO. But after
thinking about the Barnes & Noble possibility, I realized there
is a third option: Build your company under the aegis of a large
parent company that has resources you couldn't acquire on
your own.

So when is this a good deal? Make sure your potential buyer has:

1. An already-established significant customer base that could potentially buy your product
Barnes & Noble has over seven hundred stores and reaches seventy million customers. As part of Barnes & Noble, we get exposure to all those customers. And they're the same types of parenting customers we were already targeting.

2. A marketing machine and platform that you wouldn't be able to afford
Let's face the reality. Big companies have big marketing budgets, and small companies have small marketing budgets. If you play it smart, you can integrate your product as part of the overall marketing campaigns of the parent company. For example, over the summer, Barnes & Noble had a large NOOK color reader tablet campaign, and we participated in the campaign too. We developed a Tikatok app for the NOOK platform, and ran a contest on our website that we promoted in all Barnes & Noble stores.

3. Your buyer will push you to think BIG!
As a start-up, sometimes all we wanted to do is finish out the month successfully. We just didn't have the bandwidth to focus on the big picture every day. Like other entrepreneurs, we got caught up in issues like, "Can I pay salaries by the end of the month? Should I release this product now or wait until we add more features?" Guess what—big companies don't think like that. Their big question is "Can you create a multibillion-dollar business?"

A big company can challenge you to think in the same way. Are you building a product that will make an impact on millions of people? Small products marketed to small volumes are just not interesting to big companies.

The challenge to think big has really helped us. Barnes & Noble challenges us every day to take our vision and our ideas and make them bigger than big.

While many entrepreneurs resist the idea of selling their firm too quickly, there's something to be said for the bandwidth, budget, brand recognition and manpower that a larger business can provide. And if you pick the right partner, you'll still be able to think creatively, innovate and develop your own ideas.

KAY'S TAKEAWAYS

- Exiting is an important aspect of entrepreneurship. Sometimes exiting early makes sense.
- Selling to the right parent company can give you access to resources and infrastructure like customers and marketing that would take years to develop on your own.
- Working within the right parent company, you can still be able to innovate and be creative and you will be challenged to Think Big and have the resources to execute your big ideas.

WHAT TO DO WHEN YOUR VCS JUST DON'T GET IT
ELLIE CACHETTE

> *Being a trailblazer sounds glamorous, but if you're too far ahead, your investors may not be able to keep up with you.*

RAISING MONEY FOR YOUR IDEA or start-up is tough enough. As capital becomes scarce and barriers to entry become lower, venture capitalists are raising their expectations for start-ups. Here are five tips for raising money when venture investors just don't seem to get it.

1. Talk to experts.
Venture capitalists say they love disruptive ideas, but if your idea is really new, or if your industry is changing really quickly, venture capitalists might not have had time to do their homework and get caught up with you. On the other hand, industry experts will know the little wrinkles of what's going on and will be able to understand why you're different. Find these people—and the investors they work with—and show them what you're up to.

When the time comes, one start-up veteran recommends you ask these experts if they will serve as references when VCs are trying to validate or deny your company's potential. Be prepared to give your references talking points, such as details on your market and how your company fits into it.

2. Talk to other VCs or find competitors.
Another tactic is to grow a thick skin and move on. There is a common saying among entrepreneurs that it's easier to find a new investor than to change one's mind. Many start-ups raise seed and Series A rounds simply by going through the interview process. Investors are often looking for companies that match a pattern with metrics they are comfortable with. Don't waste time and energy on investors who are looking to match patterns you'll never fit.

3. Talk up numbers and educate on your space.
Sometimes it can be as simple as education—your space may have its own quirks or trends that investors don't know about. Talk up those points and break down the information into relevant points that are easy to follow. Rebecca Woodcock, cofounder of Cakehealth, was one of the first to come up with an online system to help consumers manage their health care bills. She notes, "I always have a handful of industry reports ready to send to investors to help them understand the specific trends I'm watching. For each report it's important to call out bullet points."

4. Publish a white paper or an expert publication.
If there isn't enough information out there on your niche or space, then publish it yourself. Whether it's something odd about your space, an area you plan to disrupt, or just simple statistics, you can make a SlideShare, write a white paper or collaborate with other experts in your field to cross-publish something. Show that you can be a leader in your area of expertise.

5. Find your "Esther."

Listening to early criticism of your pitch can also be huge help, and if there's something you hear a few times, you need to find a way to address it. In my case, I was frequently asked if Esther Dyson, an investor known for having an interest in health apps and software, was involved in my start-up. After being asked this a dozen times, I finally got a meeting with her and convinced her to join in. While it took some time, for me, this was a crucial step to overcoming funding hurdles. Other companies might need to convince a critical advisor or client.

Not all VCs are created equal. Many investors are excited to invest in new spaces. Break down the important information in a way that makes it easily accessible, and show that you can be a leader, even in the great unknown.

KAY'S TAKEAWAYS

- If your idea is innovative and ahead of its time, you may have additional hurdles to overcome with VCs; recruiting industry experts that VCs are already working with can help validate your company's potential.
- Educate VCs on trends they may not know about and use the industry experts to back you up. Publish expert data if it doesn't exist and establish yourself as a leader.
- Listen to the questions or criticisms that continue to come up during your investor presentations and address them powerfully.

CROWDFUNDING (AND CROWDFINANCE) 101
LUAN COX

*Here are four things you need to know before you
ask for other people's money.*

CROWDFUNDING HAS PAVED a new avenue for entrepreneurs to raise capital for their growing businesses and has generated billions of dollars for start-ups. Some do it well (think innovators such as "Generation Why Not: 35 Under 35"). Others, like New York City Opera, struggled with executing a winning campaign. New York City Opera used crowdfunding site Kickstarter to try to raise $1 million the opera needed to stay open through September 2013. It got $301,019 from the twenty-two-day campaign—not even close to its target—and filed for bankruptcy soon thereafter. Although this was not the sole reason the NYCO shut its doors (it needed to raise another $6 million from private investors but only got $2 million), entrepreneurs can learn valuable lessons from the failures of their online campaigns.

First, the NYCO did not clearly define what it was producing with the funds. Kickstarter's guidelines state that the site is not to be used for direct charity or cause funding, therefore a project from a nonprofit organization must have a clear end and focus on what is being created. Second, the campaign began a mere nine days before the 2013-14 season that it was supposed to be funding. Some thought this gave off a sense of desperation and looked like poor planning on the part of the NYCO. Both of these illustrate how lack of understanding and preparation can produce poor results in an online crowdfunding campaign.

How can you do it right? Do you even want to? Before jumping into a crowdfunding campaign, here are four things you need to know.

1. Crowdfunding is not one size fits all—you have four options.

- *Donation-based crowdfunding.* People contribute to a cause or campaign that they believe in with no expectation of returns. This is ideal for philanthropists or those wanting to support their community. Sometimes referred to as civic crowdfunding, this type of crowdfunding works best for charitable causes, community projects and other socially conscious campaigns.
- *Rewards-based crowdfunding.* A reward is given that usually corresponds with the amount contributed. Though rewards-based crowdfunding is not a new concept, it has been thrust into popularity by sites such as Kickstarter and Indiegogo. Popular with musicians, artists, movie producers and start-ups producing consumer goods, contributors are often rewarded with a prototype or some other tangible reward.
- *Debt-based crowdfunding.* This involves the person or entity essentially getting a loan from contributors and paying them back with interest. These types of

loans are growing in popularity, particularly with businesses looking to expand but not give up equity in their company.

- *Equity-based crowdfunding.* This is associated with the passage of Obama's 2012 JOBS Act, which eased federal regulations regarding fund-raising and gave individuals the opportunity to become investors in private companies. With the implementation of Title II on September 23, 2013, private companies can publicly solicit funds from accredited investors. This usually happens online through a portal such as AngelList, EquityNet or EarlyShares. When Title III is implemented, unaccredited investors will be able to invest in these private companies as well. This type of campaign entails the most legal and regulatory complexity, as it involves the sales of securities. Many project that soon this sort of fund-raising will be a vital tool for small businesses and start-ups to raise capital.

2. Crowdfunding has its own rules and regulations that you must follow.

Listing your company on a crowdfunding site may seem simple, but much regulatory compliance is required for each type of crowdfunding campaign, and a lot of legwork is involved in having a successful raise. The work on your crowdfunding campaign actually begins far before you even list your raise on a website. Social media has become a powerful (and free) marketing tool for building momentum and encouraging engagement. Take the time to develop your network; it is a personal investment in what you are trying to achieve.

However, even before you begin building the hype, you need to research the hundreds of portals out there to decide what type of campaign and site are right for you. Take your time, and make sure that you understand the regulatory compliance required for your campaign. Talk to a lawyer if you have questions, especially if you choose to go with an equity crowdfunding campaign, as consulting with a lawyer beforehand will be much less costly than paying one after something has gone awry. There are plenty of tools and resources out there to help you, such as books, blogs and videos, so take advantage of them.

3. You should not crowdfund without a business plan.
Having a proper business plan is important, especially in an equity crowdfunding raise. You want investors to know that you are serious. They want to know your priorities, and that you not only have a great idea or product, but that you have put in the time to figure out how to make it profitable. Having a good business plan can inspire the investor with confidence, trust and belief. The respective intermediary you choose may not have the most stringent requirements for posting a listing, but the more information you provide to potential investors, the better. These investors are savvy, and there are a lot of companies seeking capital; you need to stand out. Clearly explain your business goals and how you plan to achieve them.

4. You need to keep crowdfunding even after you have raised all your funds.
If your campaign is over and you were successful, don't forget that the work is not finished. Do not stop your communications afterward. Keep updating your social media with your progress, and don't lose momentum. Stay focused, and make sure that you

keep your investors informed. You will not be able to prepare for everything, but the more roadblocks you are equipped for, the better you can manage any unforeseen bumps.

Following these guidelines will help you avoid many common crowdfunding pitfalls that new businesses face when using this type of fund-raising. Choosing the right crowd-funding strategy for your business will enable you to define your capital-raising needs and the level of involvement that you would like contributors to have. Doing your regulatory homework will prepare you for the road ahead; you will not be surprised by any fees or compliances required of you. Finally, having a clear and succinct business plan will not only provide you with the framework that you need to build your business, but it will also enable you to establish your brand through social media in a genuine and professional manner.

KAY'S TAKEAWAYS

- Decide if you want a charity, reward, equity or debt crowdfunding campaign.
- Prepare your social media marketing campaign and launch in advance.
- If you choose an equity campaign, have your business plan and documents reviewed by legal advisors and be ready to go the day you launch.

CHANCE BARNETT

> *Crowdfunding is hands down the most interesting*
> *and most effective new way to find backing.*
> *Here's how to do it.*

T HIS POST ON CROWDFUNDING success tips answers
the following questions for people or businesses thinking
about using crowdfunding to raise funding:

> *"What are the common elements behind wildly successful crowd-*
> *funding campaigns?"*
> *"Which platform is the best fit for my business or project?"*
> *"What should I offer funders or investors?"*

I cover these questions and more in the following seven critical
crowdfunding success tips below.

If you'd prefer video-based crowdfunding tips on equity
crowdfunding, see the recent interview between Kay Koplovitz,
the founder of usa Network and Springboard Enterprises, and
me (youtube.com/watch?v=22DkpQc4o5s).

Crowdfunding Tip 1: Pick your platform
As you're getting started with your fund-raising and crowdfunding goals, the first place to start is to pick the platform you'll raise funding on.

To help you is a list on *Forbes* of The Top Ten Crowdfunding Sites for Fund-Raising (forbes.com/sites/chancebarnett/2013/05/08/top-10-crowdfunding-sites-for-fundraising).

First, decide if you're doing a rewards-based crowdfunding campaign, or equity crowdfunding (where people become actual shareholders in your company).

- *Rewards crowdfunding:* If you're raising rewards-based funding (not investment), Kickstarter and Indiegogo should be on your list, but you should also be aware that there are specialty platforms and communities as well that focus more exclusively on things like music, health care or nonprofits.

  It's best to pick among these rewards crowdfunding platforms based on the project types they focus on and the existing community of members already on the platform, as well as the way the platform structures their fund-raising product.

  What many people aren't aware of, or are confused by, are the differing fund-raising products and how they're structured. In short, Kickstarter has a strong track record of success for creative projects, and their fund-raising product has been an "all-or-none" fund-raising product to date. This means that if you don't raise 100 percent of your initial funding goal, you don't keep what backers have pledged.

  Indiegogo has a different product in that regardless

of whether you meet your funding goal, if you choose to pay more (up to 9 percent of funds raised), they will let you keep any of the funds pledged to your campaign. But this has its drawbacks as well, as often times projects need some minimum funding to work, and sometimes the required goal is a good incentive that motivates both crowdfunding campaign owners and those funding the campaign.

• *Equity Crowdfunding:* If you're raising investment for your start-up or business via what is called equity crowdfunding (where people actually can become shareholders for a potential future return), then check out Crowdfunder or Circle Up.

Circle Up takes a percentage of your funds raised, which according to their site is similar to how investment bankers work. Investment bankers take fees as high as 7 to 10 percent of the money you raise. On the other hand, Crowdfunder.com has a simple flat monthly fee of just a few hundred dollars.

Crowdfunding Tip 2: Pitch and story
It's important to remember the context of crowdfunding and fund-raising online. You're vying for a person's attention while they're online, and they have tons of other distractions and things pulling their attention away from you.

It's for this reason that your initial pitch and messaging absolutely must grab your funder or investor's attention right away and pull them in.

Once you have their attention, the way to keep their attention and truly engage them is to engage "the two brains," as I call it. This means engaging both the Rational Brain (the "what" of what you're doing) and the Emotional Brain (the "why" of what you're doing).

The most effective way to do this is via telling a great story—either about yourself, the story of your project or company, or the story of your customer or who your project truly has an impact on.

If you're crowdfunding a business and raising investment, there's a good resource on forbes.com on how to pitch your start-up and tell a great story and package it all in a succinct pitch deck (forbes.com/sites/chancebarnett/2014/05/09/investor-pitch-deck-to-raise-money-for-startups).

If you're creating a rewards crowdfunding pitch, you should know that videos often double success rates for rewards campaigns. You should also be sure to have a clear and compelling "ask" of your funders that relates to your larger story and project.

Crowdfunding Tip 3: Focus on what's in it for them
It may sound counterintuitive, but while your goal in crowdfunding is to raise funding for yourself, the more you can focus on what is in it for your backers or investors, the more likely you are to create a set of rewards or terms that helps you raise the dollars you're looking for.

In rewards crowdfunding, make sure you develop truly compelling rewards for your backers that tie in to your story and aren't just swag. As a rule of thumb, simply ask yourself, would I go through the trouble to buy this reward myself? Also think about what is truly and unique and compelling you could offer.

One of the best ways to come up with great rewards is to look at some of the big successful multi-hundred-thousand or multimillion-dollar campaigns. Each platform leaves the campaigns up online and you can browse through all their rewards.

In equity crowdfunding, you need to focus on what terms you're going to offer your investors. While there is not a "one size fits all" rule in raising investment, there are some guidelines to follow.

A free term sheet resource on *Forbes* is a great place to learn what your options are and what might work best for your type of business (forbes.com/sites/chancebarnett/2014/05/30/the-entrepreneurs-guide-to-term-sheets-and-equity-crowdfunding).

Crowdfunding Tip 4: Supporter engagement
The most common mistake that first-time crowdfunding campaign owners make (in both rewards or equity crowdfunding) is to not adequately engage their first-level network of friends, family and supporters.

For rewards crowdfunding, this means having people set and ready to start funding the launch of the campaign on Day 1. This is important because campaigns that accelerate more rapidly early on and attain a significant percentage of their funding goal in a short span of time often attract more attention as a whole over the life of the campaign.

For equity crowdfunding, supporter engagement more often means having important and notable stakeholders around the company online around the campaign and represented. This includes the entire team, advisors, board members, partners and existing investors. Sites like Crowdfunder.com make this easy by displaying this important "social proof" of your existing investors and team right alongside your investment offering online.

Crowdfunding Tip 5: The power of notable investors
You might believe that what you're doing is the coolest thing since sliced bread, but regardless of how great it is, there is one sure way to get other people's attention who have never heard of you or your cool gadget or project before—and that is to get people or organizations involved with your project or business who people already know and have positive associations with.

If you're involved in a rewards crowdfunding campaign, ask yourself, who can you involve in your rewards in some creative and meaningful way so that people will get excited by and respond to the opportunity to get the reward?

If you're raising equity crowdfunding, what existing advisors or investors, or even partner organizations will bring credibility and trust to you and your business?

At Crowdfunder.com, the data shows that equity crowdfunding campaigns that have notable businesspeople as investors or advisors already engaged and listed get up to six times the engagement on their fund-raising efforts as those who don't.

One of the most powerful steps a company can make is to find a first or lead investor to invest before they launch their fund-raising efforts online. This has the benefits of both avoiding the optics of $0 invested, as well as often helping to arrive at what are sometimes more "market" terms of what terms an investor would actually invest at.

The first and/or lead investor is a critical part to kicking off a successful equity crowdfunding marketing plan.

Crowdfunding Tip 6: Planned marketing and outreach
Crowdfunding platforms are not listing services. Period.

Regardless of the platform, the results you get from the platform are proportional to the effort and attention you put into the platform and tying this into your own fund-raising efforts both on- and offline.

In rewards crowdfunding, successful campaign owners put in tens to hundreds of hours on the creative and marketing planning side of their campaign before launching. They then also have a plan for several "pushes" in their marketing to launch, fund and push to close funding at or above their goal.

In equity crowdfunding, a lot of the work goes into structuring the actual investment offering by first figuring out the terms and completing all the legal agreements first. While larger investors (investment amounts at $10,000 to $200,000 per investment) aren't often effectively reached through broad marketing and PR across the web, as happens in rewards crowdfunding (donation amounts average closer to $25), storytelling and engagement are still important for both crowdfunding types.

Crowdfunding Tip 7: The data perspective
The overall crowdfunding industry is growing exponentially. In 2011, the total crowdfunding market was $1.2 billion. In 2014, crowdfunding is expected to finish off the year nearing $10 billion in funding online.

Obviously, this means that there are lots of opportunities for those seeking funding and for those who are donating, pre-purchasing or investing dollars.

But what does the data say for you as someone looking to run a crowdfunding campaign?

In rewards crowdfunding, let's say you're looking to raise $50,000. A leader in the space, Kickstarter, shared data that the most common contribution amount is $25. Knowing this, you can do some simple math to better understand what success entails.

Here's an example of what that looks like:

If all of your funding came at the average of $25 per, and you assumed a conversion rate of 3 percent of visitors who actually fund your campaign, you'd have to reach over sixty-six thousand qualified people on the web and get them to view your campaign. At the 3 percent conversion rate, you'd be converting two thousand people to fund your campaign.

For most people, that's a lot of traffic in forty-five days, and a lot of backers. Do you have the kind of existing network, reach, press contacts and marketing plan to really meet these goals?

Adding in additional higher dollar amount rewards can help. Most campaigns thus also include several higher-priced rewards from $100 up to a few thousand dollars. The point is, it is critical to "run the numbers" up front for your campaign by considering the rewards you provide and how many backers you will need to get at each reward level to make your overall goal.

Equity crowdfunding data

In equity crowdfunding, as a leader in the space, Crowdfunder .com has an average investment from accredited investors on the platform of roughly $25,000, though funding commitments from single investors and funds have been as large as $500,000.

Equity crowdfunding can provide a powerful way to raise your funding by enabling you to take fewer dollars from more investors. Let's say you're raising $500,000. At an average investment of $10,000, you'd need up to fifty investors, though most companies also get commitments in their round sized at $50,000 or $100,000, or more.

In some ways, it can be easier to find many investors at $10,000 than it is to find one or two investors at $200,000 to $500,000. The risk is just that much greater when considering investing that much money.

What entrepreneurs are finding in equity crowdfunding is that there is a new way of fund-raising now available where you can spend less time trying to convince one or two single investors over three to six months to invest. Instead, by lowering the minimum investment amount into your funding round down to as little as, say, $1,000, you lower the risk exposure for any single investor, and entrepreneurs often find it much easier to get the investment and support of many investors online at these amounts.

There's no doubt that crowdfunding is changing the rules of the game for fund-raising, and investing. Don't expect the growth or innovation to slow down anytime soon.

KAY'S TAKEAWAYS

- I only have one takeaway for this article: Read and follow this seven-step template. You'll be happy you did.

THE ULTIMATE GUIDE TO FINDING WOMEN INVESTORS
JOSHUA HENDERSON

Five insights, nine VC funds, seven platforms and lists, ten angel groups, ten accelerators, twenty articles and five tips

E ARLIER THIS YEAR, a Springboard entrepreneur came to us to say she was closing out her seed round and wanted to make room for a woman investor. Her cap table was about to be filled with male investors.

This wasn't the first time we've been approached at this point in the fund-raising game, and we have never encouraged our companies to find a woman investor just to check off a box.

Diversifying boards with women leaders has proven to help companies be more successful. Women see problems (and solutions) differently than men, and mixed-gender groups help create diversity of thought.

There's a strong business argument for entrepreneurs to diversify their cap table, not just their board and not just their management team.

Great in theory, but in practice so few people think proactively about instilling diversity at every level of their company. I want that to change.

Women investors are a small minority. I want that to change, too.

In the meantime, it will take time and it will take effort to find the right female investor who will be your partner and advocate. I wrote this guide to help make your search easier, regardless of your gender.

Five Women Investors on Finding Women Investors

1. Kay Koplovitz, Springboard Enterprises (sb.co) and Boldcap Ventures (boldcap.com)
Diversity on the cap table is ideal, as it widens the pool of human capital available to the entrepreneur. I learned with our first fund, Boldcap Ventures, launched in 2001 comprising forty-four women investors, that our value to entrepreneurs was our pool of resources that were different than those brought by coinvesting funds, which were almost entirely men. They sought us out because they began to realize that we had a network of people and resources they didn't tap into, and we sought them out for their expanded networks and ability to place follow on capital. I like to promote women as investors in companies needing growth capital, and also for broadening the pool of value-added investors on the cap table. Entrepreneurs and investors work best in combined efforts, men and women alike, and there is plenty of evidence in the market to support that position.

2. Lauren Flanagan, BELLE Capital USA (bellevc.com)
Recruiting top female investors, board members and senior management is smart business. Women account for 85 percent of consumer decisions and the majority of enterprise purchases. Women are starting the majority of new businesses and control

51 percent of the wealth in the u.s. Women-led companies are 15 percent more likely to be profitable and 30 percent more capital efficient. In the "new girl network," diversity is a given, and success pattern recognition favors female, serial entrepreneurs with the complete package: maturity, domain expertise, prior success and a deep understanding of customer, partner and collaborative team dynamics.

3. Joanne Wilson, Gotham Gal Ventures (gothamgal.com)

It is always a good idea to have both women and men on a board, as investors and in a company. Women and men look at things differently, they analyze things differently, they get involved differently, they share information differently and more than likely they bring a different network of people to the table. Having that diversity in any situation creates a balanced environment and in many ways better checks and balances. Studies have shown that having that diversity at any level in the company provides a higher chance of success.

There are not enough women investors and certainly it would be great to see more, but they are out there. There is always a balance for an entrepreneur behind passive investors and involved investors and that is diversity too. At every stage of growth, starting with funding, there are always challenges, but if you can find diversity from the get-go, meaning both men and women from investors to board members to employees, it is a very positive move in the right direction.

4. Angela Lee, 37 Angels (37angels.com)

I don't actually think that companies should try to have more women on their cap table for the sake of having more women. What I do think they should optimize for is 1) diversity of background so they're getting a mix of perspectives, and 2) investors that add value and mesh well with their working style. Having more women is one way to add diversity, but so is getting a mix of industry background, personality type and roles.

5. Stephanie Newby, Golden Seeds (goldenseeds.com)
Women make excellent early-stage investors. They are not risk averse—they want to be risk aware. Women want to understand before they write a check. For this reason, we created a series of investor training programs at Golden Seeds. Once committed, they become sought-after investors in early-stage companies, as they are typically very willing to offer their skills, expertise and connections to companies in their portfolio. They are extremely conscientious and are excellent advocates for their companies… 80 percent of the Golden Seeds investors are women. We love our male investors too. We truly believe in the power of diversity, so have welcomed men in our group since Day 1.

Nine vc Funds
Either with women partners or a track record of investing in women:

1. Women's Venture Capital Fund: Small fund focused on West Coast digital media and sustainability companies led by women. (womensvcfund.com)

2. Illuminate Ventures: Founded by Springboard alumna Cindy Padnos. (illuminate.com)

3. Aspect Ventures: Founded by Theresia Gouw and Jennifer Fonstad. (aspectventures.com)

4. *Cowboy Ventures:* Founded by Aileen Lee. (cowboy.vc)

5. *Forerunner Ventures:* Founded by Kristen Green. (forerunnerventures.com)

6. *Starvest Partners:* Founded by Jeanne Sullivan and Deborah Farrington. (starvestpartners.com)

7. *Canaan Partners:* Recognized by *Bloomberg BusinessWeek* for investing in women. (canaan.com)

8. *Scale Ventures:* Recognized by Dan Primack for the number of women partners. (scalevp.com)

9. *Springboard Fund:* Founded by Kay Koplovitz, Whitney Johnson and Amy Wildstein to invest in women-led high-growth businesses, starting with Springboard alumnae. (springboardfund.co)

Seven Platforms, databases and lists of women investors

1. *AngelList:* While AngelList is the de facto platform for angel investors, there is a dearth of women angels on the platform. There isn't a tag indicating gender, but there is a "women investors" market that lists many. (angel.co/women-focused/investors)

2. *Portfolia:* Platform of consumer-focused investors to fund women-led consumer companies, founded by Springboard and Kauffman Fellows founder Trish Costello. (portfolia.com)

3. List of Female Investors on Quora: (quora.com/Women-in-Investing/Who-are-some-notable-female-investors)

4. List of Female Angel Investors on Quora: (quora.com/Women-in-Investing/Who-are-some-of-the-best-female-angel-investors)

5. PlumAlley's Digital Database of Female Investors: Assembled by angel investor and entrepreneur Deborah Jackson. (femaleinvestors.plumalley.co)

6. TechCocktail's Femanomics List: (tech.co/femanomics-105-women-in-venture-capital-and-angel-investment-2012-05)

7. Women 2.0 list of VCs who blog: (forbes.com/sites/women2/2013/04/16/women-vcs-blogs)

Ten Angel Groups and Funds
Either all women investors or investing in women-led companies

1. BELLE Capital USA: Early-stage angel fund founded by *Businessweek* top-25 angel Lauren Flanagan to create an evergreen ecosystem of women investors investing in women-led companies. (bellevc.com)

2. Golden Seeds: Largest angel network investing exclusively in women-led companies. (goldenseeds.com)

3. 37 Angels: A community of women investors committed to funding early-stage start-ups led by men or women. (37angels.com)

4. *Astia Angels*: A global network of female and male angel investors that invests in women-led, high-growth ventures. (astia.org/content/view/337/795)

5. *Women's Capital Connection*: A regional angel fund investing in women-led companies surrounding Kansas City. (womenscapitalconnection.com)

6. *Pipeline Fellowship*: An angel-investing boot camp for women with a growing alumnae network of female angel investors. (pipelinefellowship.com/program-overview/alumnae)

7. *Broadway Angels:* An angel investment group made up of world-class investors and business executives who all happen to be women, investing in both male- and female-led teams. (broadway-angels.com)

8. *X Squared Angels*: Group of angels in Ohio investing in companies with women in senior leadership. (techcolumbus.org/technology-startup-investments/x-squared-angels)

9. *Scale Investors*: Australia-wide angel group and angel-training company focused on women-led businesses. (scaleinvestors.com.au)

10. *Launch Angels*: Early-stage firm investing in companies sourced through equity crowdfunding sites, with plans to create a fund to invest in women-led companies. (launch-angels.com)

Ten Accelerators and Coworking Spaces
Either focused on women-led companies or with a high percentage of companies with diverse teams.

1. Springboard Enterprises: Global accelerators for technology and life sciences companies led by women. (sb.co)

2. Astia: Community of experts supporting women-led start-ups. (astia.org)

3. Women Innovate Mobile: Focused on women-led mobile companies. (Each of the founders has continued to other ventures.) (wim.co)

4. 500 Women: 500 Start-ups' AngelList syndicate investing in women founders. (angel.co/500-women)

5. AVINDE: Texas-based training program for women entrepreneurs. (avinde.org)

6. Women's Startup Lab: Bay-area based accelerator and community. (womenstartuplab.com)

7. NewMe Accelerator: Virtual accelerator for diverse teams. (newmeaccelerator.com)

8. RockHealth: Health care IT accelerator with high percentage of diverse teams with a sister nonprofit, xx in Health. (rockhealth.com)

9. *Upstart Accelerator*: Accelerator for female founders and part of Global Accelerator Network. (upstartaccelerator.com)

10. *Hera Hub*: Coworking space for female entrepreneurs in San Diego. (herahub.com)

Favorite Blog Posts on Raising Capital

1. Mark Suster's six-step relationship guide to VCs. (bothsidesofthetable.com/2009/08/08/wtf-is-traction-a-6-step-relationship-guide-to-vc)

2. Paul Graham's primer on how to raise capital. (paulgraham.com/fr.html)

3. *Inc.*'s primer on how to raise capital. (inc.com/guides/2010/09/how-to-raise-venture-capital.html)

4. The difference between a VC and an angel pitch deck. (quora.com/Whats-the-difference-between-a-VC-pitch-deck-and-an-angel-pitch-deck)

5. Why it is critical to reference-check potential investors. (bothsidesofthetable.com/2010/12/14/why-its-critical-that-you-reference-check-your-vc)

6. NAV Fund's tips for a good first pitch. (navfund.com/blog/tips-for-a-good-first-pitch)

7. Mashable's tips for presenting to the full partnership. (mashable.com/2011/06/28/vc-partnership-pitch-tips)

8. Remember that it's not about what you say but how you make them feel. (blog.clarity.fm/pitching-hack-its-not-what-you-said-its-how-you-made-them-feel)

9. Have a lean strategy for raising capital. (venturebeat.com/2014/01/08/why-is-your-fundraising-process-waterfall-when-your-startup-is-lean)

10. Round up investors using one of these three fund-raising approaches. (medium.com/@twang/horses-rabbits-and-poker-boo0d1bd56210)

11. Don't get discouraged by the reality of first-time funding. (giffconstable.com/2010/05/the-cold-reality-of-first-time-funding)

12. Learn how Alexa von Tobel got funding. (businessinsider.com/learnvest-founder-heres-how-you-get-4-million-in-funding-in-4-weeks-2010-9)

13. Read how Penny Herscher raised capital. (pennyherscher.blogspot.it/2010/09/video-interview-on-raising-venture.html)

14. Lessons from Paul Stamatiou. (paulstamatiou.com/startup-fundraising-time-sink)

15. Rand Fishkin's story of the $18 million raised for SEOmoz.com. (moz.com/blog/mozs-18-million-venture-financing-our-story-metrics-and-future)

16. Angela Haines's insights on how vcs have a different way of thinking about your business than you do. (huffingtonpost.com/ angela-haines/why-pitching-investors-so_b_892333.html)

17. Chris Dixon says sell a story, not numbers. (businessinsider. com/chris-dixon-sell-vcs-on-a-stroy-not-numbers-2010-04)

18. *Inc.*'s take on the inside of a vc's mind. (inc.com/articles/ 2010/09/inside-the-mind-of-a-venture-capitalist.html)

19. The *Wall Street Journal* on the perspective vcs bring to the table. (blogs.wsj.com/venturecapital/2010/08/27/ what-is-that-vc-really-thinking-during-your-pitch)

20. In the end, remember to be yourself: All the advice in the world can only take you so far. (nea.com/blog/ recurring-patterns-be-yourself-everyone-else-is-taken)

Five Recommendations for Using These Resources

1. Do your homework.
Look at the fund's recent investments to get a sense of the regions, sectors and stages they focus on in order to better assess whether you are a fit.

2. Always go through a connection.
Find mutual connections to one of the general partners on LinkedIn and ask them for an intro. Give your connection a forwardable email under five sentences with a Dropbox link to your executive summary or pitch deck. Show you've done your homework.

3. Be politely persistent.

Investors are busy and spend a lot of time filtering potential investment opportunities. If they don't respond to your intro, don't spam them until they do. Don't give up until you get a definitive "No," but try another mutual connection, network to someone they trust and track them on social media so your follow-up pings are timely and personal.

4. Remember you need a champion.

The investor courtship occurs in stages, from first contact, to a call or meeting, to the partnership meeting, to due diligence. If you want any real shot of getting investment, you need to find your champion within the fund or angel group who will stake their reputation on you and advocate for you within the group. Make it easy for your champion to market you.

5. Don't give up.

It's going to take longer than you think, especially for first-time entrepreneurs. Recruit a "personal advisory board" to support you through the process with encouragement, connections and a dose of reality when you need it. It can be done.

KAY'S TAKEAWAYS

- Seek funding from like-minded investors.
- Determine whether the amount of capital you are raising coincides with the target range of the investor.
- Use community connections to get the right introductions to capital sources.

FIVE: INNOVATION

F OR ALL THE EXCITEMENT over the way technology
changes everything—and today, things change at a more
rapid pace than ever—there is an underbelly for entrepreneurs
that can sideline them on their way to creating the next great
company. That underbelly is innovation. To build a business
productively, one has to execute exceedingly well. One has to
combine operations with innovation to succeed in almost any
business sector today.

Entrepreneurs don't always have the experience or the
resources to build out full-grown operational talent even if they
have innovative products. Talent may be right at your side, if
you'll just take a look. Michal Tsur, cofounder and president
of Kaltura, and Leah Belsky, its senior VP of operations, offer
guidance on where to find innovation in their article, "Five
Tools for Innovation."

I know from experience that their advice to look at the talent
sitting next to you works. When I was running USA Network
and the SyFy Channel, I often used task forces to solve problems. We didn't have the budget to hire outside consultants, and
I didn't believe, anyway, that they would have more insight into
our business than the people who worked there. So I would put
together task forces made up of people from different departments and, importantly, people operating at different levels. It
was my way of seeing how people handled the collaborative

process, and who stepped up to the plate to take responsibility for deliverables. Believe me, it wasn't always the most senior person in the room who came forward. This is how I learned that new ideas come from anywhere in a company.

If you don't have all the innovation you need coming from your current team, there are great sources at universities all around the country. Julie Goonewardene offers a blueprint for successful intellectual property commercialization in her article "Finding Innovation in the Rough."

I am an example of a person with no technical background who used satellite technology to build a business. In her article, "Can't Code? You Can Still Run a Software Company," Danielle Weinblatt shares her experience in working with software engineers and how to motivate them by connecting the why instead of what they need to develop.

For those entrepreneurs who need technology, and that is just about everyone today, Joyce Durst's "Five Reasons to Keep Your Outsourcing Close to Home" will be particularly informative.

Finally, all innovation doesn't succeed. It really needs the right iterative process, customer validation and execution. Serial entrepreneur Julie Goonewardene offers advice in "Why Health Care Innovations Fail." Her clear explanations can be applied to any industry.

The pressure brought to bear today in a world of exponential growth in technology innovation and morphing business models is tough for entrepreneurs to navigate. There is less room for error than ever before. The following articles will provide insight on how to navigate these channels.

FIVE TOOLS FOR INNOVATION

MICHAL TSUR & LEAH BELSKY

Start-ups are supposed to be innovative—but they can get as bogged down in the details as any big company. Here are five ways to keep the innovative spark alive.

IT'S TAKEN FOR GRANTED that young technology companies are innovative. They're new, after all. They have new ideas and new perspectives.

Unfortunately, that's not the reality. Soon after developing their initial idea, most young companies are quickly consumed by execution, not innovation. They've got to reassure skittish customers, figure out if that new marketing whiz really deserves equity and find a health insurance plan they can afford. No wonder, then, that many start-ups lose the initial spirit and continuous idea generation that characterized their early days.

How then do growing companies stay innovative? It's a question we've been asking others in the tech community over the past year. Here's what they recommend, and what's worked for us:

1. Get some idea scouts.

You've already got these people on board—the trick is figuring out who they are and how to get the best information from them. These employees are close to users and customers, enjoy generating new ideas and know how to listen. They may be project managers or account managers, and they likely don't have much formal authority. That's okay. They're still essential. Anoint them, listen to them and make sure they're heard. They are your feet on the ground.

2. Create a task force.

Maybe you've got a great new idea, but no one to work on it. Assemble a cross-departmental team that can take a breather from their assigned duties to work through a few quick iterations of the idea. Leaders in your organization should all have the authority to call task forces together. Their goal should be to test out ideas before new projects get an organizational home.

3. Listen to industry—smartly.

In the age of TechCrunch and the ever-churning blogosphere, you can be sure that many employees are reading online all day long. But simply listening to industry gossip is not enough. Encourage your employees to read across and within your industry and to analyze the news. Why is Google entering the mobile space? Why is SalesForce now presenting itself as "social"? Encourage employees to analyze tactics in your industry and actively contribute to your own strategy.

4. The miracle of the train

Have you ever ridden a train, walked to lunch or waited in an airport with a colleague? It's amazing to witness the type of brainstorming and idea generation that can occur in these quasi-work environments. Smart leaders facilitate this type of reflection and brainstorming time. Encourage employees to travel, chat and meet together in unstructured ways.

5. *Think big.*

Insist on the importance of maintaining your company's vision. Yes, we all need to listen to customers, but it's easy to get caught up in incremental "improvements" from user requests and forget about the big ideas you started with. Identify the people in your organization who have this vision, and make sure they collaborate with those who are responding to user requests and market research.

KAY'S TAKEAWAYS

- The spirit of innovation can quickly be overshadowed by the reality of having to make important day-to-day business decisions.
- Figure out who the innovators are; listen to them. Authorize leaders to form cross-departmental task forces to test new ideas before they become part of your business strategy. Have them always hold the company's vision.
- Encourage employees to analyze innovations within your industry and to make suggestions for your company—and create informal opportunities for brainstorming.

WHY YOU CAN'T INNOVATE ALONE

DIANE ZUCKERMAN

Sure, it's fun to come up with new ideas. But do you have a real innovation? No one at your company can tell you that.

I'VE STARTED AND GROWN several health care businesses over the past twenty-five years—made mistakes, failed and succeeded. And I've come to truly appreciate a quote from serial entrepreneur Brewster Kahle: "If you want to solve hard problems, have hard problems."

Safety and risk avoidance are easy; making a revolutionary change takes guts. What does it take to win? Start with these three attributes.

Genuine innovation

Unfortunately, it's almost impossible for you to know, with any sort of certainty, that your product is innovative. For that, you need a customer. Prototyping is always an iterative process, of course. But you want to take pains to include a target customer on your team, or at least make sure your prototyping includes feedback with a would-be customer.

Think about it: Customers no longer merely consume. They want to contribute and create. Involving them at the earliest stages not only helps ensure you've got a product people actually want, but it will prove to be effective marketing as well.

Operational excellence
You need to do what you know, know what you're doing, and lead. Ideation and creativity are fun, but unless your execution is impeccable, they're not profitable. You will need a sound and detailed road map based on a clear strategy, focus and plan. At the same time, you need to respect the importance of urgency, especially if you expect to be a first mover.

Handpicked people and partners
Take care to choose the right balance of people, not just those who are book smart. You need individuals with street smarts, wicked creativity, honesty and unwavering tenacity. You want those who appreciate that every single penny spent should bring value. And, by all means, you want them to have a sense of humor.

When you're looking for partners, synergy should be the key concern. Partnerships should allow you to keep doing those things at which you are best in class, and to hand off something that is not your core strength.

Keep it simple and get the core right. You can always be a feature creeper later.

- Solving problems can be relatively easy compared to genuine innovation, which takes guts.
- In order to know that your product is innovative, you need a customer on the team at every stage.
- Choose your team carefully and your partners strategically, so that you can be best in class and execute impeccably.

*Universities can be great sources of new technology
for your company—if you know how to navigate
them.*

JOHN CHAVEZ IS ALWAYS on the hunt for the next big
idea. Literally. The president of the New Mexico Angels and
tax secretary to former Gov. Gary Johnson spends hours each
month trolling the research labs of the University of New Mexico,
visiting with scientists and their graduate assistants. John knows
universities are fertile ground for raw technology with potentially lucrative commercial applications.

"The goal is to find promising technology before it goes
public. The best way to do that is through relationships with
university researchers and the tech transfer office" at the University of New Mexico, says John. Over the past few years, he's
uncovered technologies that New Mexico Angels was able to
use as the foundation of three start-ups: Lotus Leaf Coatings,
Synfolia and Tyrosine Pharma.

John isn't the only entrepreneur or investor vetting university research. Venture capitalists routinely walk the labs
of Massachusetts Institute of Technology and Stanford University. With those two universities hauling in a combined

$142.9 million in licensing income in 2011, the VCs aren't walking away empty-handed.

So how does an entrepreneur gain access to the potentially fertile grounds of university research labs? Here are five suggestions:

Focus

There are two thousand, six hundred eighteen colleges and universities in the United States. An unfocused approach is a recipe for disaster. Home in on the industry that plays to your professional experience and knowledge base, and then identify universities conducting meaningful research in your area of interest. In software, Carnegie Mellon actively promotes its efforts and is easily a premier destination. If software is your target, Carnegie Mellon should be on your list.

Don't overlook lesser-known universities. By reading journals in your field—cancer or optoelectronics or whatever—you can quickly identify researchers worthy of a closer look based on their published work.

Do your homework

Once you've identified universities and researchers of interest, do some homework. All university tech transfer offices have websites that provide basic info. Then Google the researchers you'd particularly like to connect with. A growing number of scientists, such as Dr. Brian Benicewicz, a polymer chemist at the University of South Carolina, have comprehensive websites (benicewiczgroup.com). Benicewicz's site chronicles his career at Celanese, Ethicon and Los Alamos National Lab; describes his current research and commercial ventures; and introduces his graduate assistants—also potential sources of big ideas.

Reach out
Cultivate relationships. You could start with the university tech transfer office. These folks are paid to know what's going on in their institutions, and more specifically, in the university's research labs. Good universities won't get in the way of interactions between faculty researchers and business/entrepreneurs. Some will even broker the introductions.

Don't hesitate to reach out directly to faculty researchers. Send a friendly email inviting them to coffee. Ask to tour their lab. Ask questions and listen carefully. Just remember that the first visit is about the researcher and the researcher's work, not about you. If you encounter resistance—university researchers are stretched very thin—see the next tip.

Reciprocate
Relationships are a two-way street; if you want access to a researcher's lab, you have to bring something to the party. Without acting like a know-it-all, offer university researchers insight into potential markets, offer ways to accelerate a technology's commercialization path and offer to make introductions to potential experts, investors or resources. This will help establish you as a welcome guest rather than an unwanted time sink.

Work it
Don't expect to hit the mother lode on your first visit. Be prepared to spend time and shoe leather visiting tech transfer offices, walking labs and talking to researchers. Technology isn't going to simply fall into your lap.

There are amazing technologies being developed in university labs across the country. While university tech transfer offices maintain inventories of available IP, the advantages of going straight to the source are undeniable. Establishing old-fashioned face-to-face relationships with those generating the ideas will give you the inside track on finding that diamond in the rough. Be sincere in your interest, be willing to give advice, be consistent and just be there!

KAY'S TAKEAWAYS

- Universities can be a great source of new technology for your company and provide opportunities for investment in raw technology. Your approach to finding the right place to look must be focused.
- Do your homework, visit the websites, focus on the researchers you want to connect with.
- Focus on the industry you know, then identify the universities conducting meaningful research in your area. Cultivate relationships with those offices and faculty researchers and be persistent and consistent.

INNOVATION IS ABOUT BEHAVIOR, NOT PRODUCTS
DIANE ZUCKERMAN

True innovators get people to do new things, not just buy new stuff.

INNOVATION IS NOT INVENTION. An invention is generally a product or a process and something you can see. Innovation is different. To innovate, we must ask "why" someone does something rather than asking "what" someone does. We must design with the intent to influence or persuade, and then deliver an experience that is both meaningful and measurable to the buyer or user. That then becomes the value proposition.

Here are three important principles to consider when trying to design an innovative product, service or company:

Change is a step-by-step process.
You want to start with the commonplace and convince users to take baby steps, not giant leaps. ZocDoc started with something everyone does—calling the doctor for an appointment. The company matches requests with doctors who have open slots, and delivers the results online for easy access. Simplicity is key to change and action.

The environment shapes behavior.
The context is as important as the information we deliver. It's about changing the relationship of someone doing something. Of course the Internet has changed our behavior, but other platforms can do the same, especially those that encourage communication and collaboration. Companies such as PatientsLikeMe provide a safe and secure platform for people to share their personal experiences with their treatments, and for other patients to corroborate their experiences, become more aware of treatment options and learn from others.

Information is useless without action.
Design of your product or company should focus on a new action, not the avoidance of an old habit. A value proposition to change behavior might be "the ability for a patient to communicate and collaborate with anyone, anytime, anywhere, sharing all their own health information." This contrasts nicely with the existing paradigm, where patients are passive and wait for someone else to guide their health care. This new action gives patients confidence, control and a feel-good behavior they want to repeat.

True innovation requires a simple, personal behavioral change. A strong value proposition influences, persuades and delivers an experience that is meaningful and measurable.

- True innovation creates a change in what we do, not how we do it. It requires a simple, behavioral change. A strong value proposition persuades and delivers an experience that is meaningful and measurable.
- Start with the commonplace. Offer users the opportunity to take small steps—keep it simple and actionable.
- Design your product or service to focus on a new action.

CAN'T CODE?
YOU CAN STILL RUN A SOFTWARE COMPANY

DANIELLE WEINBLATT

I can't code, but I can run a software company.
You can too. Here's how.

A S A FOUNDER OF a software company, I often get asked about my ability to code. The answer is simple: I can't code at all.

At first, I thought what many young and eager entrepreneurs think—that I must learn how to code. So I downloaded a bunch of files to help me learn Ruby on Rails. After my first lesson, I was able to code my name forward and backward and perform simple math equations. That's about as far as I got.

But I've still been able to build a software company that reduces recruiting inefficiencies for more than two hundred and fifty companies. And I learned several lessons that are key to running a technology company without a technical background.

1. Understand the real motivations behind why people work with you.
If you can't understand what motivates your employees and what it takes to keep them happy with their careers, your organization

is doomed. In the interview process, I try to ask questions that will uncover what really motivates a developer. I can't administer a coding exam, but I can certainly try to make our work environment conducive to productivity and success.

2. Under-promise and over-deliver.
As a first-time nontechnical founder, I built credibility with my development team by promising that we would hit certain milestones such as getting accepted to an accelerator program, landing great coworking space and raising capital. I always articulated the things that we could achieve together as a team and didn't rest until I delivered what I had promised.

3. Communicate "wins" on the business side driven by innovations on the tech side.
It's easy to speak about business with your sales and marketing teams. But the development team needs to be engaged in the business wins, too. When developers see their work transformed into real revenue and happy customers, it helps build morale for everyone. Developers don't work in a vacuum, or at least they shouldn't. Business wins are rewarding for them, too.

4. Explain why things are getting done, not what needs to get done.
One of the biggest mistakes I made in the beginning was to hand developers a laundry list of features that needed to be built without taking the time to agonize over why each of these features was needed. When you can articulate the "why" rather than the "what," your developers are more likely to be in sync with the company's overall direction and vision.

I still can't code. When I asked one of my lead developers if I should learn, he urged me to focus on delivering progress on the business side and to leave development to him. I guess if we ever wanted to run simple math equations, I could step in… or not.

KAY'S TAKEAWAYS

- You don't have to code to run a software company— or cook to own a restaurant—but you do have to learn to run the business.
- Motivate your employees by building a team environment that focuses on what can be achieved together.
- Communicate your overall vision to your team, then concentrate on building the business. Leave the technical development to them—they are the experts.

FIVE REASONS TO KEEP YOUR OUTSOURCING CLOSE TO HOME

JOYCE DURST

*How to outsource your software development
without booking a flight to Asia.*

OUTSOURCING YOUR SOFTWARE DEVELOPMENT
doesn't necessarily mean you have to go around the world
in search of the right partner. Yet many managers equate well-
stocked, inexpensive talent pools with China, India or Russia.

There is another option, however, and it's closer to home.
Through our development center in Costa Rica, our consulting
firm offers so-called nearshoring. This can provide the same
cost savings as a typical offshoring arrangement, while avoiding many of the headaches that typically come with offshoring.
A well-executed nearshore outsourcing strategy can result in:

- Faster time-to-market
- A better end product
- Improved customer service
- Less frustration and fewer missed targets

Here's why we like using development teams in Central and
South America:

1. Time zones

Working across multiple time zones can create tremendous burdens for offshore development. Your software development team is often up and working while you are asleep or not in the office. When you or your offshore partner have an inevitable problem, it can take twelve hours to get an email answered, and another half-day before those responses are read. Then you often have to take a conference call outside of normal business hours.

If you use nearshoring, you can often work in the same time zone as your outsourcing partner. Phone calls and emails can be answered right away, vastly improving communication for all parties.

2. Corporate culture and expertise

Many companies based in Central and South America have corporate cultures very similar to those in the United States. Employee work habits tend to be comparable, and stable political environments reduce the risk that your project will be interrupted by a larger chaos that you can't control. The region offers a rich talent pool with plenty of engineers who are just as skilled as those in other parts of the globe.

3. Reduced turnover

Companies in countries that are traditionally used for offshoring, such as India, tend to suffer from high levels of turnover. Many nearshore options have better internal continuity, with teams that have worked together for longer periods of time. Lower turnover typically translates into greater stability and faster project turnaround.

4. Lower language barriers
Without effective communication, even the best project managers and software developers will be challenged to deliver successfully. Your organization must have a free flow of information with your outsourcing partner. Because nearshoring partners live in regions closer to home, they often have a greater familiarity with English and, as I mentioned above, with American culture.

5. Easier travel
A trip to Asia is expensive and time-consuming. It is much less burdensome to catch a plane to Central or South America. The flight south is faster and cheaper, and often allows you to stay in the same time zone.

- "Nearsourcing" in Central or South America can provide the same cost savings that outsourcing to China, India or Russia will get you, without some of the headaches and with some possible benefits.
- Central and South American companies have similar time zones and more similar cultures, with skilled engineers on par with those of other countries.
- There are fewer language barriers between South America and the U.S. Many of their workers have greater familiarity with English.
- Travel between the U.S. and Central or South America is also easier than going to Asia.

MD, MBA? *That's not what it takes to become
a health care entrepreneur.*

IN MANY WAYS, doctors are well prepared to become
entrepreneurs. They are professional problem-solvers. They
understand patient needs, and they also understand health care
trends and issues.

But for many doctors, like many of the rest of us, the trick
lies in knowing what you don't know. I work every day moving
innovation from bench to bedside, and I've found there are few
key areas that consistently get short shrift as physicians try to
build growing companies.

Market size
You can have the best idea in the world, but if only five people
need it, it's best to move on. The innovations with the great-
est potential are those that solve real problems for the largest
populations.

Dr. Mark Kyker, an anesthesiologist, noticed multiple
problems in keeping patients warm before, during and after
surgery. Cotton blankets offer no clinical benefit and must be
cleaned after use, which costs money. Electric blankets and

forced air warmers can be loud and require attachments, limiting mobility. Dr. Kyker thought the same technology used in self-heating hand warmers could be used for self-heating surgical blankets. The single-use blankets keep the patient at a consistent temperature throughout the procedure. They don't require cleaning, are noiseless, require no attachments and are affordable.

Market potential for Dr. Kyker's brainchild? With more than 51.4 million inpatient and 57 million outpatient surgeries performed in the United States annually, it's huge.

Expert advice
Starting a company requires skills not typically taught in medical school. Recognizing that you're not an expert—even if you have an MBA—is critical. Listen to those with entrepreneurial experience and use what's relevant to you.

Dr. Kyker enlisted the help of a serial physician entrepreneur, Dr. Steve Isenberg, who's also a partner in StepStone Business Partners, an angel investment firm. Dr. Isenberg and Oscar Moralez, another StepStone partner, helped Dr. Kyker found his company, Apricity, and create a business strategy.

Respect for capital
Don't expect investors to come running just because you have a great idea. Today, investors rarely look at early-stage technology. Most start-ups are self-funded with help from family and friends. If you're lucky and good, you might get funding.

The entire value chain

The health care value chain is often more complex than that of the typical start-up, particularly if your product requires FDA approval.

Dr. Kyker and his partners recognized the challenges early on and partnered with Grabber, which makes self-heating hand warmers, to help perfect the technology and produce prototypes. Apricity found a second strategic partner after a meeting with representatives of Mölnlycke, a European company that supplies a portfolio of disposable products to hospitals on a global basis, at a trade show. Mölnlycke has since signed a licensing agreement with Apricity and is now selling the self-heating blankets in Europe, giving Apricity a powerful leg up.

Failure

No one likes to fail, and physicians often associate failure with life-or-death situations. Apricity's self-heating blanket went through multiple iterations and three years of hard work before it could be successfully commercialized. The best advice is not to be afraid of failure. Get up, dust yourself off, learn from mistakes and try again. Your next idea may be the home run.

KAY'S TAKEAWAYS

- For health care professionals becoming entrepreneurs, it's important to recognize what you don't know and learn from other health care entrepreneurs.
- Be prepared to self-fund your idea during the early stages, with your own and family and friends' money. Health care innovations can be more complicated than typical ones, especially if they require FDA approvals.
- Strategic partners can be very useful in helping you develop and perfect your product or idea, and give you a better chance of getting to the finish line with it.

CHRISTINE ADAMOW

Starting and running a company in an emerging market means you need to forget some of the basic things you've learned about entrepreneurship.

I N 2006, I TRAVELED to East Africa to do consulting work with three software companies. After I became comfortable with the culture and ways of doing business in my new home, I started to see business opportunities everywhere. I soon founded Africa Biofuel and Emission Reduction (Tanzania) Ltd., an agri-biofuels company that makes fuel from the oil-bearing seed of the *Croton megalocarpus*, a tree indigenous to East Africa. Our goal is to create a commercially scalable, profitable renewable energy company.

Doing business in Africa is not for sissies. Africa and other emerging markets have the potential to bring extremely high returns on your investments of time and capital. But emerging markets also come with their own very specific, and real, risks. During my time in Africa, I've come up with three ways to lessen some of the big ones. All I had to do was forget everything I'd learned about entrepreneurship.

Think big—operate small.

Entrepreneurs are constantly urged to think big. Investors, particularly, want us to scale our businesses quickly and demonstrate that we're prepared to serve huge markets.

That's not the way to think in emerging markets. You can absolutely build a huge, successful company in the developing world. But think about it: In these places, Big is scary. These countries have a deep and profoundly negative history with Big: Big armies, Big famine, Big populations and Big droughts, to name a few. Our company gets a better response if we approach on-the-ground development in steady, small, positive steps. We keep our vision and projections to ourselves. Meanwhile, we roll out little pieces of our business model at a snail's pace, giving everyone lots of time to adjust to change.

In an emerging market, pilot programs carry the same sort of cachet that research and development carries in other places. In Africa, they don't care about our fancy R & D. They want proof that we can do business in their environment, on their terms. So we present just about any new business initiative as a pilot program. Otherwise, local and regional governments quickly start to worry that they are being forced into a long-term commitment.

Of course, time is money. You can expect your development costs to rise dramatically—maybe even to triple—because you're working in a slower operating environment.

Buy global—sell local.

Emerging markets provide great opportunities for entrepreneurs—to Western eyes, these countries need everything. The flip side is that in an emerging market, you can't just buy stuff. There will probably be no supply chain for your business. Do not try to create one, tempting as it may seem. Doing so will cost you time, money and focus. Until your company is dominant in its market, buy globally from suppliers who are already in-country and know the ropes. And bear in mind that standards for delivery, quality, service and warranties are not what you're used to. *Caveat emptor*—always.

Politics matter.
Eurasia Group president Ian Bremmer defines an emerging market as "a country where politics matters at least as much as economics to the markets." He nails it perfectly. In a country that lacks an enabling business environment, any activity with the potential to generate income and create wealth can be seen as threatening by the existing power base. You need to put a stake in the ground, communicate your terms of engagement and manage your operations very tightly. Leverage your embassy and diplomatic networks to the nines.

As an entrepreneur, you don't have the status that comes with being an operating unit of a Fortune 500 corporation. Your ambassador, your economic attaché and the State Department staff are your home office. Put them on speed dial, and make them your friends.

- Doing business in emerging markets has great potential for high profits, but they often come with high risks.
- Respect the local business environment and culture and expect your development costs to be higher because of the slower pace at which things happen.
- Work with existing infrastructure for buying supplies and keep close relations with your American embassy office, such as your ambassador, economic attaché and the State Department staff.

SIX: PRODUCT

I KNOW FROM YEARS of reading television scripts that attracting the right talent for the key roles, having the right producing team in place and then scheduling it on USA Network, a thousand and one things can go wrong in bringing a product to market. In our case, the writing could be tepid, a character might not carry the story, the arc might stray from the original direction, or the wrong talent might be cast. Many other variables can create a failure when all signs pointed to success. After all, only one in ten scripted shows survive the first season on a network, and from there the subsequent cancellations can create failure in years two, three or four.

So how did we select the winners from our slate of pilots? We didn't even have the luxury of producing as many pilots as the broadcast networks produced. We simply didn't have the money for that. We had to iterate along the way, hoping we'd attract an initial audience and build on the characters and stories the audience seemed to like most. Importantly, we had to rely on the type of show our audience came to our network for: mostly action hours with characters that could be heroes or villains, but were ones viewers were anxious to follow.

So what have our entrepreneurs learned about taking a product to market? In her article, "Liking vs. Buying: How Strong Is Demand for Your Product?" Jen Baird will provide insight on how to test the robustness of what you're offering.

Product has to move to market through the channels that can deliver to your intended market. For software and digital products that can move around the globe at the speed of the Internet, the entry point offers few barriers to getting up and in operation. But for products that are tangible, that actually have to be delivered through distribution channels owned by others, the challenges and barriers to entry can be significant. One entrepreneur, Sarah Endline, founder of chocolate company sweetriot, shares some the challenges and offers a road map to successful channel access in "How to Move Your Product to Market: Sweet Advice from Sweetriot."

How do you protect your product? Is it something that you should patent, copyright or trademark, and what does that mean for the future of your business? Does this protect your product from being stolen by others? Does it really produce a barrier to entry for your competitors? How will you know when you should take the step to protect your IP? Kelly Fitzsimmons offers advice from her own experience in her article "Ten Ways to Protect Your Intellectual Property."

In the end, products, whether digital or tangible, need to fulfill a user's pain points or fulfill their desire to have it. This is the challenge of every entrepreneur—to fill a need or create a desire to own or use the products we offer. Be mindful of everything already serving your intended market. Make sure you are adding something unique, offering some improvement or bringing something disruptive that will change a marketplace. Then protect it from competition to the best of your ability and execute, execute, execute.

LIKING VS. BUYING:
HOW STRONG IS DEMAND FOR YOUR PRODUCT?

JEN BAIRD

Customers may say you have a great idea for a product—but how can you tell if they will actually buy it?

O NE OF THE TRICKIEST THINGS about starting a company is getting an accurate read on demand. When sailors need help figuring out which way the winds are blowing, they rely on telltales—strips of fabric that flutter from the rigging. Here's how entrepreneurs can read the telltales specific to their businesses.

Is there a wind at all?
Entrepreneurs are constantly exhorted to talk to customers, and potential customers, to define a market need. Yet figuring out the best way to do that is often quite a puzzle! The first key is to focus on the potential customers' point(s) of pain: What can't they do that they need to? Why not? What is the impact?

Don't ask your would-be customers how they would solve their problems. Instead, try to thoroughly understand their pain points, and then use your expertise to invent a novel solution. Our target customers were immunology researchers. They desperately needed access to a tool called a flow cytometer or they couldn't do their research. However, the instruments available were far too expensive for most individual lab budgets. Trying to use a flow cytometer owned by a shared lab was fraught with expense and problems. It was an opportunity in the making: massive pain affecting the core of immunologists' careers, every day. The solution? A powerful, easy-to-use, affordable flow cytometer.

Is it a strong wind, or just a breeze?
Once you have identified a problem, you must test how big a deal it is. The problem the innovator seeks must be big enough and irritating enough to support your business, and something critical to the success of your potential customer. To figure out if you are dealing with a strong wind or just a breeze, look for strong positive reactions from your potential customers. For us, the telltales that we had a strong opportunity were reactions such as, "Oh, you have got to do this! How can I help?" "Please, please don't leave me out!" and "How soon can I get one?" If the reaction is, "That sounds nice," then your wind isn't strong enough.

Is it a good wind?
A strong value proposition will be essential to your future sales. Find the root causes of the customer's pain so you can understand the consequences and potential benefits of solving their problem.

Finding a robust market opportunity requires creative reading of the market winds. The strong winds are those that inspire potential customers to help you and keep in touch, so they can be first in line when your product is ready. Those are the opportunities that will open pocketbooks.

- Figure out whether your good idea for a service or product provides a solution for your target customers that they are willing to pay for.
- Test your idea out to make sure people really want it and are excited about it and that the price for your solution to relieve their pain is worth it to them.
- Understand the reasons and benefits of your solution. This will help your marketing and sales.

HOW TO MOVE YOUR PRODUCT TO MARKET: SWEET ADVICE FROM SWEETRIOT

SARAH ENDLINE

Find the product's soul, build a great team and then radiate out to the marketplace.

I HAVE SAID SINCE the beginning at sweetriot that nothing matters until you have the inside right first. For us this means two things: a fantastic team and an innovative product. In the consumer world, you can't go to market until you have this. Sales and marketing will be core of everything you do.

So first, hire right. Your salespeople represent the brand in everything you do. In any movement, they should look and feel your identity and carry the spirit. Second, it is no fun selling an inferior product, so make sure yours is a cut above. Until it is, don't launch. Enter when ready and iterate whenever necessary. I can remember an early retailer being brutally honest, and we made changes (albeit small ones) for our customers.

Once you have the team and product, it's time to "radiate to the marketplace." I think of this as having the soul right first, so you can radiate outside in an authentic manner.

So onward we go. The most important thing is to first develop a distribution strategy. This means thinking through where you want your product sold, and at what speed you want to land on retail shelves. I also ask, "Why these channels?" as it's important to think about your lead consumers. Where are they shopping and what distribution channel will reach them?

In the national organic world, many start with natural specialty stores and then slowly make their way to the leader, Whole Foods. A natural move after the natural specialty world is more regional grocery chains, such as Wegmans or Sprouts. Then you may move to national grocery chains like Safeway or Kroger.

There are other channels to consider, but this depends entirely on the type of product you have. Convenience stores (7-Eleven), drug stores (Walgreens), club stores (Costco) and mass stores (Target, Walmart) are all key players. One of the best ways to determine the proper rollout is to study those in your direct category, meaning food vs. housewares vs. beauty, etc. The Internet continues to grow as a viable channel and gives you fantastic control of the customer experience as well.

Once you have your distribution targets in mind, it's time to sell your product. As you have the right team and product in place, this may be easier than you think. You find the owners or buyers of the appropriate players and contact them. Some buy on a daily basis while others may have review periods during the year if they are larger players. These review periods are dependent on your category and tend to fluctuate. Visiting stores and customers face-to-face has been our key to closing sales—showing up with a truly passionate team and product makes a huge difference.

We have also learned that it is the "after sale" work in retail that is more challenging.

As you build out your distribution, you will need to support your product at the retail level. Promote, promote, promote. In the case of food, sampling is a core promotional strategy. This can be done in-store at demos or at outside events. Your goal is to reach your lead consumer and to convert to sales.

Another popular strategy for reaching your consumers is price promotions. Especially in a value-conscious economic environment, this is even more important. Promotions drive consumer trial.

While checking in stores, don't forget to check your shelf position and merchandising. It does matter where you are on the shelf, and it matters how many places you show up in the store.

Lastly, you want buzz, word of mouth, press and ongoing social media energy around your company and products. This means that becoming active on social media is critical, as is engaging with the press so they share your story.

KAY'S TAKEAWAYS

- Get your product right. There is no point in marketing an inferior product.
- Build the A team to develop the marketing and sales strategy.
- Choose the target market for your ideal customer and start selling.

For many start-ups, finally getting to product-market fit seems like the Holy Grail. Here are five things to keep in mind along the way.

E VERY START-UP CHASES that goal known as "product-market fit"—the semi-scientific point where a company or product reaches scalability. In our case, we had to chase down three different hypotheses before we found the one that led us to product-market fit. You can read more about our journey at slideshare.net/ecachette/journey-to-product-market-fit-16953581.

While you're working hard to find the right spot for your own product, or the right product for a market you know well, it's important to keep in mind the indicators of true product-market fit.

Business hypotheses
Make sure you're asking the right questions. For example: How much capital are you willing to dedicate per theory? That will set the tone for how you go about trying to find the right fit. Every great business starts with a business need or a solution to a problem.

Beware of false positives.

It's important to keep a neutral but open mind. It's easy to pounce on any evidence of activity as success, but first adopters are not always the best adopters.

For instance, in the beginning, a few customers may be willing to pay $100 a month for your service. But if there aren't enough of them (say, less than ten thousand) or if the expense to acquire a user is more than the amount you can charge them for three months of your service, you may not have a business model after all. It may actually be smarter to go after fewer larger clients or users.

Minimum viable product vs. minimum sellable product

If you're in the enterprise space, you may be able to sell a product that isn't built yet. But if you're going after consumers, you usually need to be able to present them with a minimum viable product.

The difficulty arises when you have a minimum product that works, but it isn't robust enough, or doesn't have enough features, for you to be able to charge for it. The question you might ask yourself is, "How far away are we from a chargeable or billable product?" If you don't know, ask potential users what they'd like to see you add, or get the opinions of those that passed.

Check your hypothesis.

How many days or weeks are you willing to spend collecting data? How long until you know you are successful? This is a refreshing framework to give yourself and your team. While some sales cycles are slow and can require months of hard work, ask yourself and your team how long you are willing to go before taking lessons learned and evolving the product.

Does your family use it or get it?

Would you use your own app? Even if it's corporate or enterprise driven? Would your aunt, mom or dad use it? If a family member doesn't use it, or can't understand it, you've got a problem. Either you're not properly communicating the value of what you're doing, or you're not solving a problem.

KAY'S TAKEAWAYS

- Achieving "product-market fit" is the goal for any start-up. It can be tricky finding the true indicators of reaching that point where you are certain you have a product that solves a problem that you can sell.
- Check and recheck your hypotheses. Know how much capital you can spend per theory, and how much time you can spend collecting data.
- You must have enough potential customers to support your model. If your family and friends wouldn't use it and can't understand it, there is a problem.

HOW TO COMPETE ON VALUE, NOT PRICE

SANDRA WEAR

Use these three steps to get customers to look beyond price to see the value your company truly offers.

I ALWAYS COMPETE ON VALUE. I will not compete on price. If you follow these three basic rules, you can do it too.

There are lots of ways to create value. Value can come from tangible factors, such as the financial return a customer gets from using your product or service, or from intangible ones, such as image or brand equity. This holds true if you're selling a product to a customer, selling equity in your company, or even selling a job to a potential hire. The fundamentals are always the same: Sell value. Don't compete on price.

Here's how:

1. Make your target customer your best friend. Make your industry your inner circle.
To successfully compete on value, you need to know everything about your target customer and your market. That includes:

- Who will be using your product or service?
- How will they be using it?

- What product or service will you be replacing?
- How does your prospect make buying decisions?
- What pain points does your prospect need to be addressed?
- What does your prospect think about your competitors and their offerings?
- How does the competition promote, price and sell its product or service?

Here's how you'll build this knowledge base:

- Read research, recent articles or posts quoting key executives on issues or challenges.
- Read press releases and annual reports from your target customers and others in their market.
- Attend events where your prospects, customers or other market players are speaking.
- Be diligent about recording information, analyzing patterns and identifying opportunities, so you can discuss them with your customers and prospects.

Yes, this is a lot of work. But the payoff can be tremendous.

2. Communicate a compelling promise that is benefit-driven.
Everyone in your organization should know the value promise. Notice I say "value promise," not "value proposition." Everyone has a value proposition, but no one does anything about it. Making a "value promise" will help focus your thinking and delivery. The promise needs to be consistently communicated in everything your company does, from marketing materials to culture to user experience.

At our company, the research described above led us to develop a simple ZigBee network setup tool. The product we developed came in two parts: a comprehensive web platform for the network manager and a simple desktop solution that offered clients a virtually automated solution for network setup. Then we changed our messaging. We were no longer selling a comprehensive solution. Instead, we promised a "1-2-3" solution for easy setup.

In making these changes, we built on our brand values of uniqueness and excellence. We established our uniqueness with our products (simple, visual rather than text-heavy, and automated), our vision (a single and standard way to control networks) and even our hiring and retention practices.

3. Deliver what you promise. If you don't, fix it.
Check in with your customers. Are they getting what you promised? If there are gaps, fix them. In another company I founded, we'd promised that our product would save clients money by reducing missed deadlines and courier costs. One particular Fortune 50 client had deployed the solution globally. They were saving money on deadlines and courier costs—but they had larger IT costs. We showed the client how we could host the software for them, bringing their IT costs back down.

- Whether you are pitching to a customer, an investor or a potential boss, sell value, not price.
- Identify prospects, what problems they are trying to solve and what motivates their buying decisions; get to know their point of view.
- Do your homework and figure out how you can position yourself above the competition.
- Promise solutions and then build your brand around the promises. Deliver on these promises and make sure your stakeholders agree you are doing so.

TEN WAYS TO PROTECT YOUR INTELLECTUAL PROPERTY

KELLY FITZSIMMONS

Companies like Facebook and Twitter show that intellectual property isn't the must-have it once was. So why are Google, Apple and Microsoft spending billions on it?

How important is intellectual property protection to your start-up? Not too long ago, defensible IP was one of the top things venture capitalists wanted to see in a start-up. But the success of several high-profile tech start-ups, such as Twitter and Facebook, that are relatively weak on patentable intellectual property, has caused many to rethink that assumption. After all, creating and maintaining a robust IP portfolio is expensive. Patents don't determine whether a start-up will be able to scale. And the lean start-up model is all about getting to market fast with the minimum viable product. Launch first, patent later... if at all.

But every start-up—lean or not—needs to plan for success. If your start-up starts to scale quickly, a strong IP portfolio will be vitally important to your ability to play the long game. The world's largest innovators, including Google, Microsoft and Apple, seem to agree. During the first months of 2012, these companies spent more than $18 billion on intellectual property in the voice space alone. They're investing top dollar to ensure that their corporate IP portfolios are diverse, rich in innovation and allow them to hedge against many possible futures.

So what should start-ups do to protect their IP assets?

- Patent what is important to others, not just you.
- Make time to get smart on intellectual property. Educate yourself and your team on the basics of trademarks, copyrights, patents and trade secrets. Investing a day or two early on will save headaches later.
- Reduce costs by doing your own IP searches first. Start with a Google patent search (google.com/patents).
- Work with an attorney who specializes in intellectual property and ask for a fixed rate to file.
- Save money by working with a patent attorney from a different geography. Ivy League lawyers in Wisconsin are just as good as Ivy League lawyers in New York City. The cost savings may be upward of 50 percent.
- Patents aren't your only asset. Conduct an audit to identify all your registered and unregistered trademarks and copyrights.
- Invest in well-written nondisclosure agreements (NDAs). Make sure your employment agreements, licenses, sales contracts and technology transfer agreements all protect your intellectual property too, right from the get-go.
- File as fast as you can. A patent application holds your place in line. You will have twelve months from

that initial submission to expand upon your filing. And remember, U.S. patents can take more than five years to issue.

- Investigate international patents if key competitors are outside the U.S. A U.S. patent will not protect you against competitors in Europe, never mind China.
- Think hard about the future. From your vantage point, what does the future look like? Use this information to devise your patent strategy, and to figure out which of your work needs to be legally protected. From there, your patent applications should flow.

As President Lincoln once remarked, the patent system adds "the fuel of interest to the fire of genius." IP rights, which include patents, trademarks, trade secrets and copyrights—even the right URLs—play an essential role in monetizing innovation. If you make it easy for others to steal your ideas, you can ultimately end up washing away your own path to success.

- Once launched, plan for the success of your company by building a strong IP portfolio, just like Google, Microsoft and Apple have.
- Educate yourself and your team about intellectual property, including patents, copyrights, trade secrets and trademarks; conduct audits and file patents fast and hire a good IP attorney from a less-expensive area.
- Invest in well-written company documents including nondisclosure agreements (NDAs), technology transfers and employment agreements.

HOW TO MEASURE CUSTOMER LOVE— AND INCREASE SALES

KAREN MOON

Have an awesome consumer product? Here are three underutilized tips to improve your sales pitch.

WHEN YOU ARE SCALING a consumer products company, scoring a large order with a retailer has obvious benefits. It helps you reach minimum orders, broadens brand exposure to consumers and serves as a marketing channel for your own website and stores.

In my past life as an investor, I have seen numerous consumer products pitches. However, rarely did I see entrepreneurs quantify how much customers loved their product and calibrate that demand.

My advice: Don't sell products—sell the opportunity. Incorporating consumer engagement data in your product sales pitch to retailers can paint the picture for the growth potential of your brand and thereby sales for your retail partners. Here's what you need to do to make this happen:

1. Utilize online consumer engagement to drive sales.
According to a recent DigitasLBi survey, 88 percent of consumers research products online even if they are making offline

purchases. Whether you are selling to a retailer for its brick-and-mortar store or e-commerce channels, upward trends in your web metrics can improve your sales pitch.

At Trendalytics, we advise brands to leverage momentum of online traffic, search queries and social media engagement to strengthen their sales pitch to wholesale partners. Free tools to measure your growth and that of competitors include Compete, Google Trends and Google Keyword Planner.

2. Promote positive customer reviews and testimonials.
A few years ago, I invested in a quickly growing headphone company. The company's financial traction was strong, but I wanted to understand how consumers perceived the products to validate its potential to expand to more retail accounts. To do this, I analyzed online customer reviews and ratings.

First, I aggregated ratings for headphones on key e-commerce sites. With a few simple calculations, I was able to determine how this company fared relative to the market. Their average ratings were in line with the top four players, and the last three essentially had the same rankings. Additionally, five of this company's skus appeared on the top twenty-five best-selling headphone products for Best Buy. Furthermore, the other top-ranked brands offered products at significantly higher price points. The facts that this company had such strong consumer efficacy and filled a price-point gap in the market were compelling. I also mined the comments for reviews that illustrated which aspects of the product consumers loved.

This headphone company ended up being one of the firm's best investments because of the outside-the-box data I used. This type of data can enhance a sales pitch to new retailers and also to increase penetration.

3. Track how many times a story related to your product or company is shared.

Retailers love seeing press articles, as it is great validation for your product. Strengthen the validation you have by highlighting the number of times the articles were shared on platforms such as Facebook and Twitter. Seventy-one percent of consumers are more likely to make a purchase on the basis of social-media referrals, so the fact that readers were passionate enough to share your story with their friends is worth touting. For print articles, mention the publisher's circulation stats to illustrate the potential reach of your PR campaigns.

KAY'S TAKEAWAYS

- Don't sell the product; sell customer engagement.
- Promote positive customer reviews and testimonies.
- Take particular note of this statement: "Track how many times a story related to your product is shared."

SEVEN: COMPANY CULTURE

O NE OF THE GREAT privileges of being an entrepreneur is that you get to establish the culture of your company. People are often not even aware of this when they start out, because they are focused on their product or service. They're so passionate about what they want to bring to market that they don't spend the time to define their own values and the way that affects the culture of a company.

I certainly knew from my work experience what kind of culture I wanted to establish when I started USA Network; I write about that in "Company Culture Is Yours to Set; Consider It Wisely." My experience seeing how employees wasted time and resources for companies led me to understand that I wanted to create a culture that maximized human capital through teamwork and collaboration.

It's important to set cultural values at the beginning of a company so you don't have to correct culture gone amok later on. I can point to numerous companies where changing company culture has taken tens of millions of investment and years to fix. Lou Gerstner, former CEO of IBM, clearly explained the painful process when transforming IBM's culture in his book, *Who Says Elephants Can't Dance*. Even for young companies, culture is hard to change, but just in case you think your company needs a cultural tweak, read Mary Jesse's article, "Three Ways to Fix Your Company Culture."

If you think trust is not a keen motivator for how employees show their commitment to your company, give them some latitude and see what happens. I certainly always felt that when you give employees some options when they run into a tough spot with a family problem or a personal issue, they will pay you back and then some by their willingness to pitch in when others need the same courtesy. You might be surprised how employees react when you read "Why We Give Unlimited Vacation Time" by Rosemary O'Neill.

Beyond setting examples, what can and should an entrepreneur do to establish the culture they want? Clearly, the first step is to understand the values you establish. It's important to write them down. Digest their meaning to you and why they are important. Then consider how you want to convey them to your colleagues, customers and stakeholders. You want them all to buy into your value creation. I can think of no more perfect example of value creation than the culture Robin Chase established when she and her partner launched Zipcar. Robin explained it at our Springboard boot camp in 2000, when she described the value each member of the car "club" was signing up for. Among the expected behavior was to return each car to its proper parking spot on time, clean, with at least a quarter of a tank of gas and ready to go for the next user. Violators of this cultural code would not remain as Zipcar users. Robin was establishing company culture as well as setting market expectations, and believe it or not, everyone buys in. The reasons for this are best told in her own words in "From the Heart: How Corporate Values Drive Authentic Brands and Customer Loyalty."

Yes, culture is an integral part of what you bring to the table as an entrepreneur. You really have to live your values for others to follow. It's important to most people to work in a culture they can buy into. Invest in creating the right culture and you won't be disappointed in the results.

COMPANY CULTURE IS YOURS TO SET;
CONSIDER IT WISELY

KAY KOPLOVITZ

*Create a workplace environment that is just the way
you want it to be, and make it one of the first things
you do.*

I LEARNED MY LESSON about company culture at the Communications Satellite Corporation in my first corporate job
after graduate school. I had written my master's thesis on satellites and their potential impact on the communications business
in 1968. Geosynchronous satellites were only put into orbit a
couple years earlier and weren't yet a part of the commercial
business we know today. So I was thrilled to secure a post at the
company leading the way for satellite launches and receiving dish
deployment in the u.s.

To a Midwest student brought up in modest surroundings,
I thought the elegant offices and people at the L'Enfant Plaza
offices in Washington, D.C., were quite impressive. Never one
to be modest about my own ambition, I thought that I would
be able to work my way up to the C suite in a relatively short
period of time. I should have realized at that time, though, that
being a retired Air Force general was a priority achievement
to be considered for the top post! Working your way up to the

C-suite floor was more akin to the military chain of command than I imagined.

Don't get me wrong. My work was pleasant enough, challenging enough, and I met people there who have become my lifelong friends and important parts of my inner circle. However, I quickly learned that the company culture at this corporation was strongly influenced by ambitious people who, I often observed, worked to undermine their colleagues in bold and subtle ways. Protecting the fiefdoms each had managed to build on their way up the corporate ladder was a top priority.

This was also the *Mad Men* culture that included three-martini lunches—not for me, but for senior guys in my department. I would often observe their office doors closed after lunch and sometimes muted snores could be heard when I passed by. What a waste of company time, I thought, but apparently it never occurred to them, and they were setting the tone.

These and other observations formed my thinking about how company time and resources are used and abused. It was then that I decided that if I were to start a company of my own, the company culture would comprise transparency, team problem solving, goal setting, cooperation and trust. I really didn't want people wasting time back-biting and playing war. I wanted a team environment where honest debates, respect for others and collaborative decision making was the rule of the day.

That's how I set up USA Network (read more at koplovitz. com/the-usa-story), based on the company culture I wanted. If an executive, support staff or any other member of the USA community didn't see it that way, they were welcome to work somewhere else. That doesn't mean people didn't sometimes have violent disagreements with decisions that were made, but it did mean that they had to argue their position with their colleagues to see if they could persuade them to theirs. I think we were pretty successful in achieving these cultural goals. To this day, I run into former employees who often tell me that their experience at USA Network was the best professional experience they ever had.

It wasn't until many years after I left USA Network that a colleague who worked with me from nearly the beginning commented that I ran USA Network like a woman. It never occurred to me that there was a difference. But we see in much research now from the attributes cited in *The Athena Doctrine* and *The Catalyst*, as well as McKinsey reports, that women lead with the attributes I described: transparency, inclusion, cooperation, respect for others, collaboration and trust, among many others. Not too surprisingly, in the social media world in which we live today, employees look for these attributes in their leaders.

I think it is important for all entrepreneurs to know that you have one chance to set the culture for your company, and it is at the very beginning. Even in those heady days of first blush business, it is important to know your values, to establish those values for your employees and to adhere to them. They define who you are and will remain for generations to come.

- As founder, you have the ability to establish your company culture.
- Set culture according to your values at the very beginning.
- Be transparent about company values and adhere to them as your company grows.

HOW TO ENERGIZE YOUR EMPLOYEES

THERESA WELBOURNE

*Meetings and performance reviews don't energize
employees. For that, you need something a little
more… random.*

As companies grow, they create routines and processes. Management seems to think this will make their companies more efficient. It might, but routines and processes also sap employee energy. And fast growth, and high rates of change, are all about employee energy.

How can you energize employees? With random moments—praising employees on the spur of the moment, doling out spot bonuses or unexpectedly paying for a nice dinner out, for example. I know this sounds counterintuitive, but the routine you probably need the most is one to create the random moments that will help energize your team. Here's how it works:

Energy is key to growth.
Energy is an internal force that propels employees to move forward and keep moving forward. Energized employees have a high sense of urgency to get things done. We can measure energy and urgency, and we can manage it.

Energy is not engagement.
Engagement leads primarily to retention. Unfortunately, high retention rates do not equal high performance. I'm not saying engagement and retention are bad, but our research shows that they do not necessarily lead to high performance. It's entirely possible to have a staff of highly engaged people, with no intention of leaving your company, who are nonetheless doing all the wrong things.

Random actions improve employee energy.
Routine, bureaucratic processes may improve fairness, but they do not positively impact energy at work. Think about it. Do more meetings make you feel more energized? More performance reviews? Of course not.

Random moments energize.
Purposefully creating random interventions helps increase a sense of urgency and our energy to move forward. The minute your practice or intervention turns routine, it starts to have diminishing effects on energy.

I witnessed just this, and was able to use it to my advantage, in my position as founder and CEO of eePulse, a technology- and data-driven human resources consultancy. Like many of our clients, we had to figure out how to redirect employees who seemed to insist on working on low-priority items. Weekly meetings and weekly reporting didn't work, but unexpected Skype calls, in which I asked employees to stop what they were doing and tell me what their priorities were, worked wonders. As long as I didn't do this regularly—as long as it was random— it was well received.

- Random acts of thanks energize employees' performance more than any routine performance appraisal.
- Random interventions such as a Skype call asking what an employee is working on yield better results than routine meetings or reports.
- The minute *random* turns into *routine*, the benefits of your practice or intervention start to decline.

THREE WAYS TO FIX YOUR COMPANY CULTURE
MARY JESSE

Scheming, back-biting and gossiping do no good.
How to put an end to it, now.

HAVE YOU EVER WORKED for a really exceptional company? For me, that company was McCaw Cellular Communications. Like many companies, McCaw had its list of company goals and values. The real difference was that everyone in the company truly embraced the culture, making a huge difference in how the company operated.

A positive company culture can drive excellent customer service, inspire the creation of superior products and help develop an award-winning workplace, all of which provide fuel for growth and profitability.

Here are three things every CEO can do to improve their company culture:

Start now.
It is very difficult to change the culture once it's embedded within an organization. Far better to set expectations from Day 1. This means proactively screening candidates for culture fit along with other key attributes. What will drive success for your business? We often want our employees to be honest, responsible,

customer-focused, flexible, innovative and efficient. Design your company's personality to be the way you want your customers to experience it.

Lead by example.
A company's culture is largely determined by the CEO. You're the one driving not only employee and customer satisfaction, but also the bottom line. As with any culture, people pick up appropriate behavior both directly and indirectly, through examples set by leaders. The CEO sets the tone for the entire organization and reinforces company culture through his or her actions. You cannot teach a concept just once if it is to be truly part of the company DNA. The culture must be reflected consistently in every communication as well as explicitly discussed periodically. Live it.

Reinforce the culture.
Nothing demotivates hard-working team members faster than seeing someone get away with bad behavior or, worse, get rewarded for it. Bad attitudes are contagious. It is always better to replace a bad attitude. This not only removes the negative influence but lets everyone else know that bad behavior isn't tolerated. Of course, you also need incentives to encourage good behavior. Celebrate success, recognize excellence and innovation, and reward those who do the right thing.

Capital is hard earned. Product development costs precious dollars. And resources and customers are like gold. Company culture is a currency available to every CEO. Don't make the mistake of overlooking it as a purely HR issue. It can make the difference between success and failure. Don't leave that money on the table.

KAY'S TAKEAWAYS

- A positive company culture can place your company ahead of the competition and improve your bottom line.
- A CEO must set the tone and lead by example from Day 1 through actions and consistency.
- Send out consistent and clear messages and incentives throughout the company that good attitudes will be rewarded and strong messages that bad attitudes won't be tolerated.

WHY WE GIVE UNLIMITED VACATION TIME
ROSEMARY O'NEILL

How will your employees react to unlimited vacation time? Depends on how you answer these three questions.

T HE CALL CAME in the middle of the day, and our COO was panic-stricken. Her husband had just fallen off a ladder and shattered his leg. Months of surgery and recovery lay ahead. Could she possibly be on a very flexible schedule for the next few months?

It took only a moment to realize that of course we trusted her to maintain her work duties, or delegate them appropriately, as she dealt with this family crisis. And the more we discussed it, the more we realized that we felt the same level of trust and respect for all of our employees.

We had very carefully hired over the years, ensuring that our team was committed, self-directed and focused. So why not put our money where our hiring was? The next Monday we announced that, effective immediately, we were offering unlimited paid leave to all employees at the company.

It was a bombshell to our staff. But it felt completely in line with our philosophy of respect and trust. If you bake in integrity and respect with regard to both employees and customers, you'll be free to spend your time and energy delivering outstanding products.

We realized there were three important building blocks that had allowed us to end up with this type of company:

1. Do you hire people, or résumés?
MBAS are great, but put a bigger priority on hiring people with the right attitude and outstanding communication skills. How can you evaluate these during a job interview? We ask each candidate to write (with a pen, on paper) a one-page essay in fifteen minutes. You'd be surprised to see what you can find out about someone using this simple technique. Asking a fairly senior person to do this task will either result in semi-offended compliance, or a smile of surprise. Hire the one who smiles and is still busy writing when you come back into the room.

2. How open are you to feedback?
The respectful organization is constantly accepting and giving feedback within the team. There's a collegial atmosphere in which systems are flexible, rather than set in stone. If everyone agrees on the destination, then it's easy for everyone to move toward it without micro-management. Our regular supervisor-employee check-ins are designed to measure contributions to corporate goals, not hours worked. If deadlines are being met, products are being shipped and customers are happy, then I don't care if half the staff is surfing on Friday afternoon.

3. Do your employees create fiefdoms?
Every employee should have well-defined goals, and the freedom to accomplish them. That means that the marketing and the technology folks should know what's coming up for each other.

When we once had a repetitive, simple coding task that had to be done on a schedule, we cross-trained a couple of non-geeks and got it done in short order. You need to create a business in which colleagues can support each other without getting wrapped up in job descriptions and titles.

Building an atmosphere of respect goes far beyond implementing a single policy or perk. It is a pervasive corporate value, built from the ground up.

KAY'S TAKEAWAYS

- Unlimited vacation time is a possible perk for your business if you trust and respect your employees, believe the feeling is mutual and have created the type of company that can support this.
- Identify and hire people who will support each other across departments and job descriptions.
- Giving unlimited time off as a perk to employees is only one possible expression of a companywide philosophy of mutual trust and respect.

NOT JUST ANOTHER NOTEBOOK
CANDICE BROWN ELLIOTT

Scientists' laboratory notebooks have illustrious histories—and deserve a shot at the future.

O NE OF THE FIRST things I did, upon founding my first company, was to buy a bunch of laboratory notebooks imprinted with our firm's name. Each new employee was issued a numbered notebook and personally instructed as to how to document his or her work, especially innovations or inventions. This included the receptionist.

I had two reasons for doing this. First, I wanted to reinforce the idea that intellectual property development and protection was a key component of our firm's business plan, and that we took it very seriously. Second, it sent the message that everyone's ideas had value to the company. No exceptions.

Too often, a company's corporate culture creates expectations about whose ideas will be heard and whose won't be. How many companies expect—truly expect—their receptionist or their shipping clerk to suggest the inspired idea that leads to the next blockbuster product? Thirteen years after Clairvoyante, mine does.

The lowly notebook does not often get the respect it deserves. We think of notebooks as repositories for nearly illegible meeting notes, appointment dates and to-do lists. These are all necessary functions, of course. But the noble laboratory or inventor's notebook is in another league altogether. Leonardo da Vinci's paintings might still be in our leading museums, but would his name be known by nearly everyone if not for his notebooks filled with illustrations and text describing his ideas on flying machines?

Attending Fairchild U

My first job as an engineer was at Fairchild Semiconductor. It's called Fairchild University for a reason: It's known for the number of firms founded by its alumni. On my first day, I was issued a numbered laboratory notebook. My new boss, C. C. Wu—the man who invented the matched dual operational amplifier in the early days of the integrated circuit—showed me how to use it.

Writing in that notebook became a very strong habit. I took pride in the neatness of my entries, the workmanship of my illustrations, the clarity of my thoughts. The discipline of a well-written entry forced me to think through my ideas and their implications. Each time I made a new entry, I had a senior colleague read it over and then sign and witness each new page.

This was not some perfunctory review. My colleagues questioned each idea, in detail, until they understood exactly what I was attempting to document. I came away with new ideas for further research and better skills as a writer, with a new ability to more clearly state what might have started out as only a vague idea. I will be forever grateful for this early discipline.

When I moved from Fairchild to Advanced Micro Devices, I was again issued a numbered laboratory notebook. But, surprisingly, I wasn't given any instruction about how the notebook should be used. The act of assigning the notebook was just another task on a checklist that the human resources department rushed through for each new hire.

Months later, as I prepared for my first patent application, AMD's attorneys complimented me on the quality of my documentation. Over the next several years, those attorneys used my notebooks in training sessions for both new and longtime employees.

In thirty years, I've filled volumes of lab notebooks. I've been told that such notebooks will soon be a relic of the past, and will go the way of manual typewriters. Now we write up our reports on laptops while sipping our second mocha. When we're done, we hit send and entrust our writings to the vagaries of the local Wi-Fi hotspot. I'm even told that the whole reason for an invention notebook—the need to prove priority—is no longer valid. The United States has joined the rest of the world, granting priority by "first to file" rather than "first to invent."

Yet I remain the anachronism, sitting in the corner of a café, with my pen hovering above the pages of yet another notebook, marshaling my thoughts to renewed clarity before committing them irrevocably to paper, and perhaps to prosperity.

- Protecting intellectual property by keeping detailed documentation in a notebook may seem tedious and time-consuming, but it will be worth it if you ever need to defend the ownership of your work.
- Notes will show organization of ideas and will credit the person with patent filing.

THREE KEY TRAITS OF GREAT ENTREPRENEURIAL HIRES
ALEXANNDRA ONTRA

Just because someone was a star at a big company doesn't mean they'll shine for you. Here's what to look for.

WHEN IT'S TIME TO HIRE, many of us have the same instincts: Look for Fortune 500-level company experience combined with a prestigious education.

No doubt those candidates offer a wealth of experience and contacts. But on many levels, it's easier for someone to succeed when they have the resources and branding of a large company behind them. Think of John selling Nabisco cookies compared to James selling Granny's Best Chocolate Chips out of a makeshift kitchen. Both John and James can put in the exact same amount of time and effort, but you can bet that John will sell more cookies and make more money. If John transitioned to Granny's Best, would he be successful? Maybe, if, in addition to his pedigree, he shows the following:

Flexibility
Look for employees who are flexible in both thought and action. Smaller and newer companies often reinvent themselves over and over again, as they define their market and their product

offering. Their employees must be willing to put aside their alleged job descriptions, roll up their sleeves and switch gears as the company's needs dictate. They need to be as nimble as the company itself.

Humility
There is nothing more humbling than getting tripped up over tasks that, in a previous job, an underling used to do for you. A friend of mine with an Ivy League MBA recently moved from a senior position at an international packaged goods conglomerate to a senior position at a tech start-up. She has the knowledge, skills and contacts to succeed in her new environment, but she became ridiculously frustrated after spending five hours fumbling with fonts and images for a PowerPoint pitch. The content was spot-on, but the slides looked awful. Her comment was simply, "I had an assistant do that for me!" But she sucked it up, persevered, sent her deck to her client and closed the business. Not everyone with her credentials would bother with menial tasks they considered to be beneath them.

Creativity
Such a trite word. But what is it? The ability to think out of the box; to make something out of nothing; to make lemonade out of lemons. However you define it, a start-up requires employees who can think for themselves and excel without a lot of process and spoon-feeding. Small companies lack the protective layers and systems (bureaucracy) that slowly grow their employees and compensate for any one person's weakness. Some people will sink without structure. Others will thrive; they love the intellectual freedom and challenge. Hire the latter.

The challenge for the employer is that these traits are difficult to qualify in a résumé or job interview. But they are critical to success within a start-up. Ask a candidate to describe situations in which he or she had to act quickly, solve a problem or change course. Then listen between the lines to how they reacted in the situation. Do they tell their story with pride and excitement? Or is it laced with negativity and resentment? You want the positive attitude.

KAY'S TAKEAWAYS

- Skills needed for entrepreneurial businesses may be different than those required or learned at big corporations, where support staffs are prevalent.
- Flexibility, humility and creativity are needed to succeed in start-up businesses in addition to the contacts and experience learned in corporate careers.

FROM THE HEART: HOW CORPORATE VALUES DRIVE AUTHENTIC BRANDS AND CUSTOMER LOYALTY

ROBIN CHASE

Draw in your customers with transparency and authentic core values and your customers will become your best advocates.

MARKETERS TRYING TO CONVINCE customers that a company is value-driven and cares about them when the CEO and the corporate culture don't match that reality have a difficult task. Over time, cracks will appear and the lack of authenticity shines through.

When one of my daughters moved to a new school, she told her fellow third graders that I was raising eight foster kids in addition to my own three, and that her father was a professional ice hockey player. Not. At one point, she admitted to me: "It gets harder and harder to remember the details and keep it all straight." Indeed.

Back when I was founder and CEO at Zipcar and establishing the brand, we'd do periodic customer surveys, comprising both quantitative and qualitative elements. My favorite free-form response, which we actually got several times, was: "Everything you say is true." And it was.

As CEO, I deeply believed in the benefits of the service, in the general goodwill of our members (who we had to trust to treat the cars well), in being transparent about our shortcomings and fixing them quickly, in being a learning organization, and in recognizing that it took teamwork (customers included) to produce the Zipcar service. A good customer experience was thanks to the efforts of everyone all along the chain: website design and writing, a simple and straightforward application, a reservation system that took seconds, cars that were consistently outfitted and well maintained, helpful and sincere customer service, great marketing and business development. Every employee understood that what they did mattered, was valued and was integral to the whole.

I took Zipcar's core principles and turned them into one word so that we could all remember them: SCREACH. Zipcar sought to be simple, convenient, reliable, economical and environmental, admirable, customer and community focused, and humorous (that is not how you spell "screech"). This mnemonic was an easy way to keep us on track.

Zipcar members were part of this team, an idea that is increasingly accepted today but was totally novel back in 2000. As such, we would genuinely ask members for advice on all sorts of things. Sure, some of the engagement was for fun and to generate participation (What shall we call the next car? Come to our holiday cookie-swap party), but it was also sincere (Want a job? Do you know of any good parking spaces? Where shall we expand to next?).

Storytelling in routine emails proved very powerful to communicate our values to members. As a side benefit, employees read them as well. The storytelling was an important part of culture creation and branding: Here's what we think is funny, interesting, amazing; here is what we do; here are our challenges; here is how we treat people and talk to our customers; we admit mistakes. And I always tried to tell a story that someone would want to repeat. Zipcar grew virally because at every touch point, the customer was surprised and delighted and went on to tell someone else about it. Customers couldn't help but talk about us.

KAY'S TAKEAWAYS

- Authentic messages ring true with customers. Be true.
- The CEO needs to drive the authentic message through the organization straight through to the customer.
- A satisfied community drives social marketing success.

S TRIKING OUT ON YOUR OWN to be an entrepreneur doesn't mean you have to go it alone. Today there is an infinite amount of advice and instruction available for free. In addition to free access to everything from boilerplate term sheets to competitive metrics in your marketplace, you can learn from webinars on everything from iteration processes to securing patents. The Angel Capital Association is a good source of information, and so is the Kauffman Foundation.

Some of the most valuable resources might be your future competitors and, without a doubt, people sitting across the table from you in any number of meetings may offer valuable advice. Whether you're marketing your product or service or raising funding, the customers, lawyers, venture capitalists and accountants who work with early-stage companies could offer you priceless advice.

Chapter Eight offers a view from across the table. Springboard advisors and investors offer you advice from their own playbooks. Pay attention to what Cal Hackeman has to say about presenting your financials to potential investors in his article, "Why Some Ideas Get Millions and Others Get Zilch." Be sure you understand your own financial models and the assumptions upon which they are constructed. No one's financials at an early stage or in a high-growth business ever prove to be totally correct. The things I pay closer attention to are the assumptions upon which the financials are built. This is where an investor gets insight into the CEO's thinking about how to build the business. Understanding the assumptions and accessing them to be valid is one way potential investors can size up a deal.

Lauren Flanagan offers her perspective on what investors want to see before investing. In her article, "Seven Things Investors Love to See," she sets forth her checklist for investing. Lauren is a GP in BELLE Capital, is on her third investment fund and is often cited as one of the leading angel investors in the country. She knows how to judge investment-grade companies, and entrepreneurs should take her advice seriously. Ask yourself, "Can I meet these standards?" If you can't, keep working on your business until you do, to give yourself the competitive advantage you'll need when vying for investor dollars.

You will find more valuable advice from Pamela Contag, serial entrepreneur and a board member of Springboard in her article, "Five Ways to Close the Deal." Kelly Fitzsimmons, also a serial entrepreneur and investor, shares her experiences with strategic investors, especially learning to read how they think. Many entrepreneurs underestimate the amount of time and number of resources it takes to get deals done with large corporations. Kelly gives advice from hard-won experience on how to cement that deal.

Practical advice on compensation issues is offered by Jessica Catlow, an attorney who specializes in employment law. Knowing the regulations setup in your state of business can save you costly lawsuits from disgruntled employees later on. Ellen Corenswet, a longtime advisor and lawyer for dozens of early-stage companies, takes you through what you should know about term sheets before you set out on the process of fund-raising.

Last, but not least, Dana Ardi shares her vast experience in shaping the management teams of legions of high-growth companies in her article, "Seven Predictions for the Future of Work." She has condensed this information from her acclaimed book, *The Fall of the Alphas: The New Beta Way to Connect, Collaborate, Influence—and Lead.*

Take advantage of what these experts share with you. Find out what they're thinking. Many have benefited from their experience, and many more would have if only they had access to their clear thinking. It is my hope that you will be among the fortunate who will benefit. I wish you all success in business and life. And when you achieve your goals, please come back to us and share your wisdom so those who follow will share in your knowledge. Pay it forward: That is the Springboard way.

WHY SOME IDEAS GET MILLIONS, AND OTHERS GET ZILCH

CAL HACKEMAN

> *If you want investment, you need to learn investor-speak.*

ENTREPRENEURS COME UP WITH gazillions of great ideas every year. They all require financial capital, as well as human capital, to become successful businesses. Obtaining that financial capital is one of the biggest challenges of being an entrepreneur.

So why do some ideas get millions of dollars of investment, and others get nothing?

Speak investor.
One part of the answer to that question lies in how you present your financial forecast to your potential investors. You need to present a compelling financial case for them to invest, just as you present a compelling case for the need for your idea and the likelihood that it will achieve market acceptance. Your financial forecast should have enough specifics to be credible but not so much information that your potential investors lose interest as they wade through spreadsheet after spreadsheet. The numbers you present must comply with generally accepted accounting

principles, because one day you will have to compare your actual financial performance to the forecasts in your pitch packet. That should be an apples-to-apples comparison.

How much financial information is enough? What is too much?
As a potential investor, I want to know what you are going to do with the capital I give you, and what I can expect to receive as you use that capital to turn your idea into a business. I don't need to know the details of how you are going to spend every dollar.

Start by thinking about your business. Which activities are critical, and how much revenue will they generate? I suggest grouping the critical activities the way you will manage your business and then preparing your financial forecast using those categories. As a rule of thumb, if an activity is not going to require more than 5 to 10 percent of your expenditures, or if it is not going to generate 5 to 10 percent of your revenues, it probably doesn't need a separate line in your financial forecast. Instead, lump those expenditures or revenues together with a similar category.

Make sure your financial forecast is on solid ground.
Do not assume that cash coming in or going out of your business will result in revenue or expenses, respectively. When it comes to financial reporting, accounting and cash flow are very different things. Your potential investors will want to know your forecast for both. They will be the first to point out the errors of your ways if you tell them they are going to be the same.

Revenue is a particularly challenging and important number in your financial forecast. Make sure your financial advisor knows how your business should recognize revenue in accordance with generally accepted accounting principles, and prepare your forecast on this basis. If you and your financial advisor aren't sure, seek professional guidance from a CPA who has other clients in your business.

Presentation can make all the difference.
One of my pet peeves is financial forecasts that supply exact dollar amounts (e.g., $169,478 of marketing and sales expense) out into Year 3. If you are that good at predicting the future, you should probably skip going into business and just predict the future for a living.

Rounded amounts (e.g., $169,000) give your potential investors all the information they need and will help them stay focused on the big picture. I would also avoid truncating your financials ($169K or worse yet, $.169M) in the early stages of your business and capital raising. Truncating will come later when your sales and operations are so large that the amounts no longer comfortably fit in your financial results.

Forecast a reasonable profit within a reasonable period of time.
Potential investors are expecting to earn a return on their investment. They are taking a risk by investing in your idea and they expect to be rewarded for doing so. If your financial projections do not show revenue growing faster than expenses after the initial start-up phase, you probably should rethink your business model.

On the other extreme, the "hockey stick" growth curve is tough to achieve and most likely not realistic in today's economy. If you are projecting hockey stick growth, you will need to be prepared to defend it with very convincing and reliable market data. Remember, you are starting or growing a business, not a charitable organization. That means you should be forecasting a reasonable profit within a reasonable period of time.

Make sure it all syncs.
Finally, make certain that your financial projections are in sync with the language you use to describe why an investor should give your idea serious consideration. If you say that there is a huge market for your product or service, your financial projections should show that you are going to capture a reasonable share of that market over time and do so in a way that provides capital for future investment and provides a return of capital to your investors.

After you finish your financial projections, put them away for a day or two and then take them out and look at them without the rest of your pitch packet. Do your financials tell potential investors what you are going to be doing and how you are going to do it? Do they present convincing evidence that will entice an investor, or do they just raise a lot of questions as to what your business model is all about? Hopefully they are convincing, not confusing, and will add to the excitement your would-be backers already feel.

KAY'S TAKEAWAYS

- Prepare clear and concise top-line financial projections.
- Make sure your assumptions are in sync with your business storyline.
- Be prepared to speak confidently about your financials. Investors want to know that you understand the proposition you are offering.

SEVEN THINGS INVESTORS LOVE TO SEE
LAUREN FLANAGAN

Want investors to take your start-up seriously?
Here are seven things you need to do.

R AISING START-UP MONEY is never easy. For women, minorities and entrepreneurs located between the coasts, it can be like weightlifting on Venus.

These seven proven strategies will help elevate your start-up in the eyes of potential investors.

1. Field a strong core team.
Investors bet on the jockeys. If you can recruit top talent on a shoestring, that shows you've got leadership ability. Investors also look for domain expertise, and for prior entrepreneurial experience among the founding team. Teams that have worked together before are preferred—this should not be your first rodeo. Likewise, teams that have generated prior successful exits for their investors generally get funded more quickly and at higher valuations.

2. Fill an unmet need for a billion-dollar market.
Investors look for "must-have" rather than "nice-to-have" solutions to big market problems. Big markets mean that you have

room to succeed despite mistakes, and that your solution will be more attractive to potential acquirers. Make sure to accurately calculate your addressable market, and to build sales projections from the bottom up. Statements such as, "This is a $3 billion market, so once we get 5 percent of it, we'll have $150 million in revenues," just aren't credible. Few companies achieve even 1 percent market penetration.

3. Fill the gaps in your management team with experienced board and advisory members, and use the best professional service providers.
A good start-up board has three members: the CEO, a seed investor representative and an independent industry expert. The latter two should be making customer/strategic partner and investor introductions. Your advisory council should comprise a mixture of industry and domain experts.

Adding successful entrepreneurs can also give you invaluable insights and cachet. Sign them on for two to three years and pay them with stock options. Engage top law firms (general and intellectual property) and financial advisors (CPA, taxes, auditor). Forming a strong board and hiring top professional service providers shows investors you know what you're doing, and showcases your value proposition before you can pay much in the way of fees.

4. Demonstrate sales traction with your reference customers.
Nothing smells like success to big-name customers like sales. If your product or service is still being tested, sign market-leading customers to paid pilots, get them to agree in advance to success metrics and ask them to serve as references for investors and other potential customers.

5. Form strategic partnerships that give you competitive advantages or economies of scale.
The best capital is the capital you don't have to raise. Seek transformative partnerships that help you get to market faster, distribute more widely or manufacture more cost-effectively. Then structure a deal that tightly weaves your start-up into the fabric of your partner.

6. Show how your business will make money and achieve scale.
Investors want to know how they will make money. Eighty percent of investor exits come from mergers or acquisitions of less than $200 million; 50 percent are under $50 million. Early-stage investors want to make ten to twenty times their investment within five years. Show how your start-up will make money, how it will scale, and cite investments in comparable companies at comparable stages to illustrate the potential returns to investors.

7. Develop a detailed financial model and capital plan.
Build your financial model from the bottom up. Try to project monthly cash flows for the first two years, and quarterly cash flows for the next three years. Estimate how much cash you will need to get to each major value driver before you reach cash flow break-even. You need to be able to answer the key investor question: How much total capital is required to get your start-up to exit?

Make sure you're targeting investors interested in your market segment, but don't let "no" slow you down. Your skin will get thicker and your pitch more persuasive. Keep on hunting until you find the right investor fit.

- Build a strong team of managers, advisors and strategic partners.
- Fill the need of an unmet market that can support your business to scale.
- Show investors how you will make money for them.

FIVE WAYS TO CLOSE THE DEAL

PAMELA R. CONTAG

When do you just need to hang in there, and when are you being strung along? Some tips to get you on the right track.

OVER THE LAST EIGHTEEN YEARS, I have been inside almost every Big and Small Pharma company pitching a deal of some sort for one company (my own) or another (not my own).

Some years ago, I had a very cool technology that would fit perfectly into another company's product. I contacted the CEO, who agreed with me, and we set out to do our due diligence and, hopefully, close the deal.

While we came to an early understanding of how the companies fit together, the specific terms of the collaboration seemed to take forever to work out. As the months dragged on, I thought daily about calling it quits, but pinged the company weekly in hopes of getting to a quicker close. There was even a time when my CFO said, "Let's at least threaten to walk." My response was, "Rome wasn't built in a day."

Each week we made some progress, especially on the trust side. The timeline stretched to nine months, during which I was told that they loved the deal and were motivated but needed more time to work on it internally.

At the end of the sixth month, it finally happened. We heard that the delay had nothing to do with us but everything to do with internal financials. Our patience was rewarded. We got the terms nailed down and signature pages completed. Threatening to walk away would have ruined the trust between us. The deal turned out to be a great opportunity for both parties, as I originally envisioned.

That experience has guided me through all my subsequent transactions, including the road show for my initial public offering, the sale of my company and the raising of capital for several businesses.

Here are five things I have learned about closing deals:

Start every deal with a clear view of how both sides benefit by knowing the core business.
This, to me, is always the hardest analysis. You need to know what the value of the deal is. You can't ask for less than the project is worth, of course, but overreaching can also kill a deal. Sometimes the added value of the deal is intangible. I try to paint a picture for all showing just that.

The hardest deal to close is the one that you need to stay alive.
Never believe that one lost deal will be the downfall of your company.

Work to build trust.
Get to know the people you will be in business with and, more importantly, how they work best. Posturing erodes the trust you have built.

Patience is a virtue.
No matter how much you want the deal to close quickly, deals always take time, patience and an understanding of what the person on the other side of the table is dealing with internally.

Don't be biased by your contact's title. Remember that even if the person across the table isn't the final decision maker, they will likely be your first internal champion.

Deals never happen quickly or the way you originally envision. But if you approach them in the right way, patience, honesty and trust can go a long way.

KAY'S TAKEAWAYS

- Start the process by knowing how each participant will benefit from the deal.
- Build trust among the parties. When the negotiations get to the final strokes, some decision makers rely on trust to close the deal.

STRATEGIC PARTNERSHIPS:
THE VIEW FROM THE OTHER SIDE

KELLY FITZSIMMONS

As an entrepreneur, your partnership with BigCo might be the most important thing your company has going right now. Chances are BigCo doesn't see it that way.

F OR SOME ENTREPRENEURS, this is the dream: Find a tiger—a large, global company that can provide sales, distribution and branding for your product or service—and ride them to the promised land.

What the entrepreneur often fails to see, of course, is how this relationship looks to the tiger! We picture ourselves as important, helpful, a meaningful contributor. But to the tiger, we may be a flea, an annoying gnat or just a chatty spider monkey bouncing up and down for attention.

To avoid being ignored or worse, eaten, the entrepreneur needs to understand the tiger's perspective.

Beth Bronner, managing director of Mistral Equity Partners, has a tiger's perspective. She spent decades as an AT&T executive, guiding multiple strategic partnerships. Bronner is blunt: "It is unusual that the partnership is as important to the global player as it is to the start-up." That's not to say the partnership doesn't have value, Bronner emphasizes. "Large companies need help with creative solutions. They often have problems with innovation and need the partnership."

She advises start-up entrepreneurs to cultivate patience—a trait often lacking in the average start-up CEO (self included)—and be ready to wait. By planning long lead times into any partnership plan, you can avoid the pitfall of being too optimistic too early.

In March, I participated in a panel discussion about strategic partnerships hosted by the State University of New York Levin Institute. Here's what I've learned—from my own experience, from Bronner and from my fellow panelists.

1. Large, global companies are not nimble and tend not to move fast.
Don't set the relationship up to fail by insisting on unrealistic deadlines or trying to convey a false sense of urgency.

2. When waiting for a response, try not to go around your contacts.
Chain of command matters, and someone who feels like you've attempted an end run can easily get you blocked from the account.

3. Be prepared!
Come to your meetings armed with detailed questions that will help you quickly assess how the partner has worked in the past with other start-ups similar to yours.

4. Do not give out too much information too early.
Invite more interest by providing tantalizing tidbits and highlighting the possibilities.

5. Make sure to get the right nondisclosure agreements in place early on and have them reviewed by your attorneys.
Without diligence here, you can give up valuable rights and even intellectual property in the NDA.

6. Make it easy for your sponsor to help you.
Clear and direct requests show that you are considerate of their time and understand their pressures.

7. Be likable.
People help those they like. And if you don't like them, chances are that they don't like you either. Find a new contact or move on. Otherwise, you are wasting your time.

8. Your sponsor is only one window into the organization and may not be aware of forces working against you.
Try to triangulate your relationship quickly as possible in parallel. (See No. 2.)

9. Share good news along the way, and do it often.
A partner will be more interested if they can see tangible progress over time.

10. Cultivate a pipeline.
Partnerships work a lot like customer acquisition. Not every one works out. Make sure that you have multiple partners at the table.

11. Do your homework.
If you show up asking basic questions about your partner's business, consider the relationship over. Fortune smiles on the prepared.

- While you may value a partnership with a big global brand, you will not be as important to them as they are to you, so be patient.
- Large companies are generally slow. Allow for long lead times.
- When meeting with your contacts at the firm, come prepared and be considerate of their time. Do your homework.
- Make it easy for your sponsor as the partner to help you. Be clear and concise when making a request.
- Cultivate relationships and share good news. Be likable and respect the chain of command!

THE TWO BIGGEST PAY MISTAKES YOU'RE MAKING— AND HOW TO AVOID THEM

JESSICA CATLOW

Looking at employment laws now will save you headaches later.

YOU HAVE YOUR GREAT IDEA, your business plan and some seed capital from friends and family; now you are ready to build out your team. At this critical stage, often overlooked are the various rules governing the employment relationship, especially around compensation. This oversight then comes back to haunt you when potential investors are kicking the proverbial tires during your first major capital raise and they want your company to make representations and warranties regarding the company's compliance with various compensation and employment laws.

These are two common mistakes made by start-ups. Avoiding these can spare you from unnecessary headaches and save money:

1. Don't misclassify employees as independent contractors.
One of the most common practices of small companies is to engage a host of "freelancers," sometimes referred to using the misnomer "1099 employees," because, oftentimes, the company

cannot afford to have dedicated full-time staff. However, just because you call someone a "freelancer" (and they agree to be so called) does not mean they are not considered employees in the eyes of the law.

Employers are required to withhold income, Social Security and Medicare taxes from employee compensation, pay unemployment taxes on wages paid to employees and provide state workers' compensation coverage. Employers are not required to do so for properly classified independent contractors. If you misclassify an employee as an independent contractor and fail to make these required withholdings and tax payments, your company could be subject to penalties, interest and back taxes.

The Internal Revenue Service and most state agencies use a twenty-factor test to determine whether a person is properly classified as an independent contractor. The factors focus primarily on behavioral control, i.e., the "when, where and how" in providing the services. The IRS and state agencies view the classification narrowly, and the general assumption is that the individuals are employees.

Unless you are engaging someone to perform a discrete one-time project or provide a service unrelated to your business (think of the contractor painting your new office space), it is usually a better practice to assume that the individual should be classified as an employee.

2. Don't fail to pay certain employees overtime pay.
Another common mistake made by young companies is to pay their employees on a salary rather than hourly basis, and assume that, because they are paid a salary, those employees are not entitled to overtime pay.

Under both federal and generally all states' laws, employees are entitled to be paid time and a half for all hours worked over forty in each work week, unless they are properly classified as executive, administrative or professional employees. Whether the employees fit into one of these categories and therefore are not entitled to overtime pay depends largely on the nature of their primary duties. Generally, only employees with authority to make independent decisions over matters of significance are properly classified as exempt from overtime. You should carefully consider whether an exemption is available for a particular employee. Failure to do so can be costly: Federal laws and many state laws will award punitive damages and attorneys' fees, in addition to the unpaid overtime, on wage claims brought by employees.

I know you have many things to focus on in your venture but, as the saying goes, an ounce of prevention is better than a pound of cure. It's better to get it right in the beginning than pay the consequences down the road.

KAY'S TAKEAWAYS

- Decide whether to classify workers as independent contractors or employees.
- Determine which employees must be paid overtime.

TEN THINGS YOU SHOULD KNOW ABOUT TERM SHEETS FOR EQUITY FINANCING

ELLEN CORENSWET

> *Raising money, even in the best of funding environments and with the hottest idea, is time-consuming and challenging.*

THE TERMINOLOGY—"pre-money," "priced round," "Series A," "participating preferred"—is like learning a foreign language. Valuation alone may not be the most important measure of the best term sheet.

And you're supposed to learn and handle this successfully while you're growing and running your company.

The following tips should prove helpful in navigating the equity financing arena, particularly in your first professional angel or venture capital round.

There is no one size fits all.
What is a good or bad term sheet will depend on a number of factors, including the stage of the company, the nature of the existing and new investors, the credentials of the management team, the "hot" fundable ideas du jour, the amount and terms of funds you've raised to date and the investment environment.

Raise enough money to take you to the next valuation inflection point.

Fund-raising is tremendously time-consuming and you will almost always need more money than you think to get to the next stage. How much funding do you need to achieve one or more milestones that will truly make your company more valuable in the next round of financing?

Evaluate the proposed valuation in the context of the entire term sheet and the quality of the investor.

The highest valuation may not be the best overall deal. And a high valuation can lead to unhappy investors if the next financing is at a lower valuation. Also, if you have the luxury of choosing among lead investors, consider who will make the best partner to work with going forward—who shares your vision, really understands the space, shows enthusiasm and trust.

Build your own pro forma cap table showing post-deal equity ownership. Include the cap table in the term sheet.

This will help you understand the impact of the proposed economic terms on management and existing investors and will reduce the chance of a misunderstanding between the company and the investors regarding how the proposed terms actually work. The cap table should include an equity pool reserved for employees and other service providers that is adequate to attract the necessary talent to take the company to the next level (typically 10 to 20 percent of total shares).

The principal factor affecting "real" valuation is the liquidation preference.

Is the preferred stock participating or nonparticipating? Is the participation capped? Prepare a model of how the proceeds of a sale of the company would be split among the equity holders at different sale prices.

Control of the company is driven by the terms of the investment documents, not just the percentage ownership.

Investors will have veto rights over later financings, a sale of the company and certain other actions, no matter what percentage they own. Also, the agreements will address investor representation on the board of directors and may dictate the "slots" for the entire board and board committees. Try to build a balanced board of directors, including industry experts who are neither management nor investors.

Do your own diligence on the investors while they do theirs on you and the company.

What is their industry knowledge and network, their "dry powder" for later rounds? How have they conducted themselves with other portfolio companies?

Pick your issues.

Don't negotiate every term. Make sure you understand what each proposed term means, whether it is "standard" and what the alternatives are.

Understand the role of the CEO/founder in the term sheet negotiation.
As CEO, you are negotiating on behalf of the company (your
stockholders/members), not on behalf of yourself. You can—
and should—make sure you are adequately incentivized, but
that is a separate and parallel negotiation. Note that employment
agreements are rare in early-stage companies.

*Engage an experienced lawyer to assist the company in the
transaction.*
Your "friend" or "personal lawyer" may be the closest to you and
the least expensive on an hourly basis, but having a lawyer who
has handled numerous venture transactions and represented
numerous emerging companies will, in the end, make the transaction go much more smoothly and at a lower overall cost.

KAY'S TAKEAWAYS

- There is no one size fits all in term sheets. Be
  prepared to modify according to stage of offer,
  valuation and investor's appetite.
- Valuations are tough, but equity and terms are
  equally important.
- Understand that as CEO you are negotiating for the
  company. Separately, have representation for yourself before completing the deal.

KICKED OUT OF YOUR OWN COMPANY: WHAT TO DO
SUSAN STRAUSBERG

*It happens more than we admit: Entrepreneurs get
kicked out of their own companies. What to do when
it happens to you.*

As the cofounder and CEO of EDGAR Online, I ran
the company for thirteen years. For the vast majority of
that time I was fully focused on the development and growth of
the company and firmly committed to remaining the CEO until
I felt we'd achieved our vision. But after a very desirable acquirer
backed out, my investors grew restless and pushed for a succession plan. Two months later, I was informed by the board that
the succession plan had been accelerated and that our president
would now be the CEO.

This sort of scenario happens far more often than either
entrepreneurs or investors like to admit. Here's how, when the
time comes, you can be prepared:

Write your succession plan.
Whether your company is public or private, make sure you have
a succession plan and that your interests are protected. Assume
that your separation agreement will have a noncompete clause,
and make sure you understand the terms of it. The noncompete

should relate to your company's business specifically, and should not prohibit you from other types of ventures. Even if you live in California, where most noncompetes are unenforceable, you don't want to be heading to court just as you're being ousted.

My noncompete restricted me from engaging in ventures in financial information, which was entirely reasonable. I had stock ownership in my company and it was in my best interest for the company to continue to thrive. Also, in reality, broad or overly general noncompetes rarely hold up in court, so it is in both parties' interests to be clear and fair.

Keep a stiff upper lip.
When the rug gets pulled out from under you, you have to somehow keep it together. You have to immediately come to terms with the decision and behave with extreme dignity that befits the legacy you plan to leave. Above all, as unpleasant as it can be, you need to understand that you anticipated this and participated in the succession process.

When it happened to me, I called a trusted advisor for input and sympathy. His first question was, "Did you cry?" I said, "No," and he congratulated me, saying that is the thing people fear most about women CEOs. (Great.) His next question was, "Are you going to stay on the board?" That's an important question, because as long as you remain on the board, you are subject to regulations concerning purchases or sales of stock in the company. You're also setting yourself up for some pretty uncomfortable meetings. I remained on the board until it became absolutely clear that my input would either be ignored or worse.

Get out of Dodge—at least mentally.
You need to get a new perspective immediately. A fresh start will give you a sense of relief, which you will certainly need. I started a new venture, and we decided that New York was not the right place to do that. The conditions of my noncompete, plus my pride in EDGAR Online, made it impossible to engage my original founding team. We moved to Austin, Texas, where we felt the environment would be more supportive.

Yes, you could do it better. Forget it.
Don't stress over the problems of your former company. Maybe the stock is tanking and the new management is clearly clueless. You can't do anything about it. Think about it this way: You want to concentrate on the new company, in which there are a myriad of things you actually can control.

Ask yourself this: Are you as passionate about your next innovation as you were about the previous one(s)? Are you driven to look forward, not back? Can you apply everything you learned at that earlier company to make your next one even more successful? The opportunity to feel the rush of a start-up is not limited to your first company. It's the gift that keeps on giving.

- Once investors are involved, the board's plan for growth of your company may include removing you as CEO. Be prepared to execute your succession plan with grace and understand the terms of your separation and noncompete agreements.
- Understand that it will be a difficult time, but that you knew this might happen. Move on and through it as quickly as possible.
- Move on! And do something that drives you forward so you won't be looking back.

*Everything you thought you knew about the
workplace is already outdated.*

G ONE ARE THE DAYS when decisions were made from the top down and when all anyone was expected to do was simply "their job." As a corporate anthropologist, I study the cultures of organizations—how they evolve and intersect with what's happening right now, and how the people in them influence and shape their communities. Here are a few changes you should be preparing yourself and your business for.

The talent pool will grow.
As the use of robotics and automation technology increase, humans will no longer be asked to perform rote tasks. That means the nature of jobs will change. Greater connectivity means we will have greater access to talent literally all over the planet.

A new form of labor pool and market where individuals, project teams, or even entrepreneurial companies (that are really just teams of teams) from all over the world will bid on high-value tasks and opportunities. This new dynamic will not only increase the efficiency of organizations, it will also change the notion of what "managing" means. It will also create competitive pressures for organizations to embrace global languages and cultural awareness as a way to appeal to the most talented workers.

Collaboration will be the norm.
The type of company—and people—that will thrive in this new environment will embrace collaboration and teamwork. I call them the Betas. The old-fashioned Alpha way of doing business—top-down, command-and-control—will no longer be viable.

As Alpha methods die out, employers will be looking for innovators, technologists and big thinkers. Data managers will remain in high demand as will people with the skills to manage a diverse workforce.

"Limited contracts" will rise.
As we move into a craftsman and service economy, people will work for organizations for two to four years with incentives built in to compensate them for the level of impact they bring to the organization.

Specialization will be even more essential.
The flatter and more networked the workplace becomes, the more essential it will be for people to continually build their skill set and maintain a level of specialization that enables them to stand out in a crowd of talent.

Social networks will become a way to partner.
Workers at all levels will need to market themselves through their social networks, forming partnerships and gaining influence by striking deals based on their deep skill specializations.

Everyone will become an entrepreneur.
People will work for and with many clients and partners simultaneously. At the same time, individuals will have greater control over the kind of work they tackle and how they are compensated.

Individual contribution, not pay grade, will be rewarded.
With a more peer-to-peer network in place, individuals stand to reap greater rewards than in the more inefficient hierarchical systems of the past where those at the top of the pyramid paid themselves first. Rewards will be tied to the value of an individual's contribution and not to any artificial title.

I write about the rise of this new kind of organization and workforce in my book, *The Fall of the Alphas*. The future of work will be different than it is today and, as the old adage says, fortune favors the prepared.

- The talent pool will grow with teams of people inside and outside corporations.
- Everyone will become an entrepreneur, selling skills.
- Social networks will become the connectors of work engagement.
- The ability to continually market yourself will determine success.

AN APPRECIATION OF
MURIEL "MICKIE" SIEBERT (1928–2013)
FOUNDER, CHAIRMAN AND CEO, SIEBERT FINANCIAL

AMY MILLMAN

"TAKE STANDS, TAKE RISKS, TAKE RESPONSIBILITY."
That was told to me by the "First Woman of Finance,"
Muriel "Mickie" Siebert, who grew up in Cleveland and left in
1954 to seek her fortune in New York City. She drove a used
Studebaker and brought with her $500 and a goal to make it
on Wall Street. Along the way, she had to "kick open the driver-
side door," she said, in order to get out. Mickie never stopped
kicking open doors, including the door to the New York Stock
Exchange, where in 1967 she became the first woman to buy
a seat.

Mickie, as she was known to all of us, was a woman of many
firsts during her epic career. She was the first woman to own her
own firm with a seat on the NYSE, first to launch a discount bro-
kerage firm on the first day members were allowed to negotiate
commissions. She was the first woman to be superintendent of
banking for New York State, and first to battle the sexist and
anti-Semitic practices then prevalent in New York social clubs.
She was a first for me as well: my first mentor.

Even when she was the first in the door, she always held it
open for other women, no matter how few chose to follow. The
fact that it took more than ten years for another woman to join

her at the New York Stock Exchange really aggravated her. "For ten years," Mickie said, "it was one thousand, three hundred sixty-five men and me."

Being a "market disrupter" is a lonely and often futile pursuit. During meetings of the National Women's Business Council, a commission I ran in the 1990s and on which Mickie served, I remember her interjecting, "It's taking too long."

There was no road map, no sorority of support and no female role models to pattern herself after, so she just blazed her own path. It took her only a decade to figure out that she needed to start her own firm and two years to secure the money to buy her way into the NYSE. Yet almost fifty years later, women are still waiting for an invitation. We would be wise to adopt her brazen strategy for dealing with social and professional obstacles: "I put my head down and charge. When you hit a closed door and it doesn't open easily, don't get discouraged. Just remember my Studebaker. When all else fails, just rear back and kick the door open. But don't do it just for yourself—do it also for those who follow you."

CONTRIBUTORS

CHRISTINE ADAMOW is CEO/director of Africa Biofuel and Emission Reduction (Tanzania) Ltd. She brings more than twenty years' experience founding, managing and operating start-up and early-stage companies. She founded eCent Technology Inc. in 1998 and served as its president through 2003. She is a Springboard alumna.

ERIKA ANDERSEN is the founding partner of Proteus, a consulting and training firm that focuses on leader readiness. She serves as coach and advisor to the senior executives of such companies as GE, Time Warner Cable, TJX, NBC Universal and Union Square Hospitality Group. She is a Springboard advisor. @erikaandersen

DANA ARDI, PHD, has served as a partner/managing director at CCMP Capital and at JPMorgan Partners, and was a partner at Flatiron Partners. She is the founder of Corporate Anthropology Advisors and the author of *The Fall of the Alphas: The New Beta Way to Connect, Collaborate, Influence—and Lead*. She is a Springboard advisor.

SUSAN ASKEW was cofounder and CEO of Backfence.com, one of the first citizen-generated, hyperlocal content web companies.

She also founded womenCONNECT.com. She is a Springboard alumna. *@susanaskew*

JEN BAIRD is CEO of Accio Energy Inc., an early-stage company that is defining a new direction in wind energy generation. She is a Springboard alumna.

LESLIE BANE is the director of marketing at Hara Software Inc., a leader in enterprise software for energy and sustainability management. She founded SEN-CE in 2008 and served as COO/VP, marketing until 2010. Leslie is a Springboard alumna.

CHANCE BARNETT is an Internet entrepreneur, investor and advisor who has started and bootstrapped several companies from inception to millions in revenues over the last sixteen years. He is founder and CEO of Crowdfunder. *@chancebar*

LEAH BELSKY is senior vice president of operations of Kaltura, provider of the world's first open-source online video platform. She is a Springboard alumna.

DENISE BROSSEAU is the CEO of Thought Leadership Lab, a Silicon Valley-based executive talent agency. She cofounded Springboard Enterprises and serves on its advisory council; she founded the Forum for Women Entrepreneurs and the Invent Your Future Conference. *@thoughtleadrlab*

ELLIE CACHETTE is VP, product marketing, at Koombea and known as an expert in product-market fit and product design. Before that, she was the founder of ConsumerBell, a software company focused on product recalls. She is a Springboard alumna. *@ecachette*

JESSICA CATLOW is an employment attorney at Mintz Levin. She represents both companies and executives regarding executive compensation issues in the context of mergers and acquisitions, venture capital investments and private equity financing. She is a Springboard advisor.

ROBIN CHASE is the founder and CEO of Buzzcar, a peer-to-peer car-sharing service. She is cofounder and former CEO of Zipcar. She also started GoLoco.org, an online ridesharing community. She is a Springboard alumna. *@rmchase*

PAMELA R. CONTAG, PHD, is founder and CEO of Cygnet Bio-fuels. She is a founding board member of Startup America Partnership. A Springboard alumna, she serves as a director of Springboard Enterprises and is on its national advisory council.

ELLEN CORENSWET is the cochair of the venture capital/emerging company practice group at Covington & Burling LLP. She is on the board of national advisors of Springboard Enterprises Inc. and has been a longtime advisor to Springboard companies in the tech, media and life sciences sectors.

LUAN COX is the CEO and cofounder of Crowdnetic, which provides technology and data solutions to the global crowdfinance marketplace. She is also an alumna of the Springboard Accelerator program.

JOYCE DURST is cofounder of Austin-based Growth Acceleration Partners (GAP). She was the CEO and president of Pinion Software, a security software company. She is a Springboard alumna.

CANDICE BROWN ELLIOTT is founder and CEO of Nouvoyance, an independent fabless semiconductor firm, developer of PenTile Subpixel Rendering technology. She is a Springboard alumna.

SARAH ENDLINE is CEO and chief rioter of sweetriot, which sources in Latin America, features artwork on all of its healthy organic products and sells in places like Whole Foods and Virgin America. She is a Springboard alumna.

KELLY FITZSIMMONS is the cofounder and CEO of HarQen, a next generation web-telephony company. She is a Springboard alumna.

LAUREN FLANAGAN is managing director at BELLE Capital USA, an early-stage fund that targets women-led tech companies in underserved markets in the U.S. A Springboard alumna, she is a board member of Springboard Enterprises and serves on its national advisory council.

SHARON FLANK is founder and CEO of InfraTrac, a product verification company. She spent ten years at SRA International, where she wrote the company's first patent and helped create companies later sold to AOL and Kodak. She is a Springboard alumna.

JULIE GOONEWARDENE is associate vice chancellor for innovation and entrepreneurship at the University of Kansas. She cofounded and served as president and CEO of Cantilever Technologies, a venture-backed software company. She is a Springboard alumna.

CAL HACKEMAN is a retired partner of Grant Thornton LLP, where he served as the national managing partner of the technology industry practice. He sits on the board of directors and is treasurer of Springboard Enterprises.

BETTINA HEIN is the founder and CEO of Pixability, a video marketing company. She cofounded the Swiss-based speech software specialist SVOX AG. She is a Springboard alumna.

JOSHUA HENDERSON is the vice president of Springboard Enterprises. He writes about relationships, networks, start-ups and capital at joshuahenderson.com. *@joshuahenderson*

MARY JESSE is a wireless industry expert with more than twenty-five years of experience developing and operating wireless solutions. She is CEO of Ivycorp, developers and operators of Ivytalk, an enterprise messaging solution. She is a Springboard alumna. *@ivytalk*

SHARON KAN has founded four start-ups, among them Tika-tok, built from its foundation with a group from MIT. She is a Springboard alumna.

KAY KOPLOVITZ cocreated Springboard Enterprises. She is the founder of USA Network, the Sci-Fi Channel and USA Networks International. She is chairman and CEO of Koplovitz & Co. LLC.

RENEE LORTON is president and founder of White Rock Advisory, providing board and advisory services to early-and mid-stage technology companies. She is a Springboard alumna.

AMY MILLMAN is cofounder and president of Springboard Enterprises. She is on the advisory board of Enterprising Women Magazine and Dell EIR.

KAREN MOON is cofounder and CEO of Trendalytics, a visual analytics company that measures how fashion and beauty trends resonate with consumers. She is a Springboard alumna. @KarenMoon140

ROSEMARY O'NEILL is cofounder and president of Social Strata Inc., which makes the Hoop.la online community platform. She is an alumna of Springboard Enterprises. @rhogroupee

ALEXANNDRA ONTRA is cofounder of Shufflrr, a presentation management solutions company that organizes, updates, distributes and tracks PowerPoint content. She is a Springboard alumna.

JULES PIERI is founder and CEO of the online marketplace Daily Grommet, her third start-up. She is a Springboard alumna. @julespieri

CAROL POLITI is president and CEO of TRX Systems Inc., which delivers mapping and location indoors, underground and in other areas where GPS is not reliable. She is a Springboard alumna.

LAURA MCCANN RAMSEY is associate partner at The Parker Avery Group. She has been senior vice president, product management, for Stylesight, the online trend service. Laura is a Springboard alumna.

LYNLEY SIDES is CEO of The Glue Network, a platform that enables companies of all sizes to improve their bottom lines through giving and social media. She is a Springboard alumna. *@LynleySides*

SUSAN STRAUSBERG is cofounder and CEO of 9W Search Inc., a next-generation financial search platform optimized for mobile devices. She is a Springboard alumna.

LAURA STRONG, PHD, is president and COO of Quintessence Biosciences, a cancer-drug development company. She is co-author of fourteen publications and coinventor on four issued patents. She is a Springboard alumna. *@scientre*

MICHAL TSUR, PHD, is a cofounder of Kaltura Inc. and is its president. She is a Springboard alumna. *@michts*

SANDRA WEAR is an entrepreneur who designs and implements scalable growth strategies to maximize shareholder value. She is founder of the tech companies DocSpace Company and Atalum Wireless. She is a Springboard alumna. *@sandrawear*

DANIELLE WEINBLATT is the founder and CEO of Take the Interview. She is a Springboard alumna.

THERESA WELBOURNE, PHD, is the FirsTier Banks Distinguished Professor of Business and Director of the Center of Entrepreneurship at the University of Nebraska, Lincoln. She is the founder, president and CEO of eePulse, a human capital technology and consulting firm. She is a Springboard alumna.

MARCIA ZELLERS is vice president and head of operations at Stradella Road, an L.A.-based marketing strategy and digital services agency. She created and runs Tootzypop, a blog for urban women over forty. She is a Springboard alumna.

DIANE ZUCKERMAN founded Evidence-Based Solutions and is in a partnership with Asia Pacific e-Health Group (APEHG) in Singapore. She is a Springboard alumna. @dzEBSol

Copyright page information continued...

The following material originally appeared on inc.com:

"Ten Signs You're Ready to Quit Your Day Job," Kelly Fitzsimmons; "How to Sell Your Ideas," Denise Brosseau; "Bootstrapping: Five Tips," Ellie Cachette; "Where Are All the Women Entrepreneurs?" Denise Brosseau; "How to Write a Pre-Nup for Your Partnership," Laura McCann Ramsey; "Trapped in a Big Company? What's an Entrepreneur to Do?" Marcia Zellers; "Lead So Others Will Follow: Six Tips," Erika Andersen; "How to Lead from the Middle," Kay Koplovitz; "Why 'Urgent' is Not a Priority," Laura Strong; "Get More Time to Think: Four Tips," AlexAnndra Ontra; "Five Ways You Can Promote Women's Leadership," Kelly Fitzsimmons; "How to Be Pregnant and CEO: Five Tips," Bettina Hein; "How to Get the Most out of Your Advisors," Jules Pieri; "Brainiacs for Your Business," Sharon Flank; "Three Ways to Expand Your Future," Denise Brosseau; "How to Make Social Responsibility Work for Your Company," Lynley Sides; "Are You Ready to Raise Money? How to Tell," Carol Politi; "Six Steps to a Perfect Pitch," Renee Lorton; "Finding the Right Investor," Ellie Cachette; "Is It Time to Pivot? How to Tell," Leslie Bane; "Nope, Your Investors Can't Help," Susan Askew; "When It Makes Sense to Sell Your Company Early," Sharon Kan; "What to Do When Your VCs Just Don't Get It," Ellie Cachette; "Crowdfunding (and Crowdfinance) 101," Luan Cox; "Five Tools for Innovation," Michal Tsur and Leah Belsky; "Why You Can't Innovate Alone," Diane Zuckerman; "Finding Innovation in the Rough," Julie Goonewardene; "Innovation Is about Behavior, Not Products," Diane Zuckerman; "Can't Code? You Can Still Run a Software Company," Danielle Weinblatt; "Five Reasons to Keep Your Outsourcing Close to Home," Joyce Durst; "Why Health Care Innovations Fail," Julie Goonewardene; "Taking the Risk out of Doing Business Overseas," Christine Adamow; "Liking vs. Buying: How Strong Is Demand for Your Product?" Jen Baird; "Five Tips for Getting to Product-Market Fit," Ellie Cachette; "How to Compete on Value, Not Price," Sandra Wear; "Ten Ways to Protect Your Intellectual Property," Kelly Fitzsimmons; "How to Measure Customer Love—and Increase Sales," Karen Moon; "How to Energize Your Employees," Theresa Welbourne; "Three Ways to Fix Your Company Culture," Mary Jesse; "Why We Give Unlimited Vacation Time," Rosemary O'Neill; "Not Just Another Notebook," Candice Brown Elliot; "Three Key Traits of Great Entrepreneurial Hires," AlexAnndra Ontra; "Why Some Ideas Get Millions and Others Get Zilch," Cal Hackeman; "Seven Things Investors Love to See," Lauren Flanagan; "Five Ways to Close the Deal," Pamela R. Contag; "Strategic Partnerships: The View from the Other Side," Kelly Fitzsimmons; "The Two Biggest Pay Mistakes You're Making—and How to Avoid Them," Jessica Catlow; "Kicked Out of Your Own Company: What to Do," Susan Strausberg

The following material originally appeared on huffingtonpost.com:
"Leadership Requires More Feminine Attributes," Kay Koplovitz; "How Do I Find the Right Mentor?" Kay Koplovitz; "Stiletto Network: The Emerging Power of Women's Human Capital," Kay Koplovitz; "Company Culture Is Yours to Set; Consider It Wisely," Kay Koplovitz

The following material originally appeared on forbes.com:
"Seven Crowdfunding Tips Proven to Raise Funding," Chance Barnett

The following material originally appeared on joshuahenderson.com:
"The Ultimate Guide to Finding Women Investors," Joshua Henderson

The following material originally appeared on LinkedIn:
"From the Heart: How Corporate Values Drive Authentic Brands and Customer Loyalty," Robin Chase

The following material originally appeared on corporateanthropologyadvisors. com:
"Seven Predictions for the Future of Work," Dana Ardi

CPSIA information can be obtained at www.ICGtesting.com
Printed in the USA
BVOW02*0127151015

422398BV00002B/17/P